Piaget's Theory:
A Primer

Piaget's Theory:
A Primer

John L. Phillips, Jr.
Boise State University

W. H. Freeman and Company
San Francisco

Sponsoring Editor: W. Hayward Rogers
Project Editor: Pearl C. Vapnek
Copyeditor: Linda Purrington
Designer: Marie Carluccio
Production Coordination: Ron Newcomer & Associates
Illustration Coordinator: Audre W. Loverde
Compositor: Graphic Typesetting Service
Printer and Binder: Arcata Book Group

Library of Congress Cataloging in Publication Data

Phillips, John L   1923–
    Piaget's theory.

    (A Series of books in psychology)
    Bibliography: p.
    Includes index.
    1.   Piaget, Jean, 1896–   2.   Cognition.
3.   Cognition in children.   4.   Knowledge, Theory of.
I.   Title.
BF311.P523P48   155.4'13'0924   80-20800
ISBN 0-7161-1235-0
ISBN 0-7167-1236-9 (pbk.)

Printed in the United States of America

9 8 7 6 5 4 3 2 1

```
THANK YOU  PLEASE

      COME AGAIN


··3      *   1 18·84   *



····   2 I      ··0.40   *
····   4 *      ·10.25   *
····   4 *      ·13.95   *
····     *      ··0.03   TAX
····     *      ·24.63   TOTL
····     ☐      ·25.00   CASH
7350A17:34      ··0.37   CNG
```

To Greg and Jeff

Contents

Preface

This book presents a general summary of Piaget's theory of intellectual development from birth through adolescence. It is intended for persons who have had no previous acquaintance with the writings of Piaget. Much of Piaget's thinking is difficult to follow, but readers of my previous attempts to interpret his theory have encouraged me to believe that it can be understood by people who have had no training in psychology.

Piaget's Theory: A Primer incorporates suggestions volunteered by numerous students and instructors who found my earlier book, *The Origins of Intellect: Piaget's Theory,* to be useful. Readers familiar with that book will find that I have borrowed from it freely, abbreviated the discussion of some topics, and omitted others entirely.

This volume includes some innovative interpretations of Piaget's notion of representation. Concepts pertaining to representation are among the most abstruse in his theory. I have endeavored to render them intelligible by providing sections entitled "Figurative and Operative Aspects of Thought," "Relations Between Figurative and Operative Aspects of Thought: 'Memory' as an Example," "Consolidation of Concepts: A Working Vocabulary for Beginners," and "Summary of the Semiotic Function." In some cases I have noted redundancies in the vocabulary that Piagetians use to refer to those representational concepts, and in all cases I have emphasized the relations that exist among them.

In the interest of efficiency, the first chapter functions as both introduction and summary. It should be used also for reference as needed while reading the remainder of the text, for all of the most important concepts are there in close proximity to one another. Anyone who takes advantage of those features should emerge from the experience with a good basic comprehension of Piaget's theory.

Because the theory is inherently difficult, it is important that no unnecessary difficulties be added by the language used to present the ideas. In general, wherever nontechnical language is appropriate, I have tried to be as accurate as possible, using the English vocabulary of an educated person; and where technical language is appropriate, I have tried either to define each new term or to use it in such a way that its meaning is clarified by its context. I have used the first person ("I" instead of "the author") and the second person ("you" instead of "the reader") freely throughout the book because that usually is the simplest way of saying what needs to be said. I have used the generic masculine ("he" instead of "he or she") for the same reason.

It is my hope that *Piaget's Theory: A Primer* will lend itself to use as a text or supplement for many courses in child development, as well as any course in which the instructor wants students to get a brief but illuminating exposure to this famous theory.

Acknowledgments

I am indebted to Margaret Donaldson, of the University of Edinburgh, and Hans Furth, of the Catholic University of America, for their critical readings of the new material on representation. I am also grateful to Constance Kamii, of the University of Illinois, and John Renner, of the University of Oklahoma, for their thought-provoking letters on many topics related to Piaget's theory.

September 1980   *John L. Phillips, Jr.*

Piaget's Theory:
A Primer

1

Introsummary

1

1

Introsummary

*As its title implies, this chapter is intended to serve two functions: an intro-
duction and a summary. It is an introduction because you need a working
knowledge of basic concepts in order to comprehend subsequent accounts of
the developmental periods and to appreciate their significance. It is a summary
because you will find that, when you reread it after having studied the other
chapters, loose ends will tend to fall into place.*

*Incidentally, it will be much easier in that second reading; so don't panic
if everything is not clear the first time through. Do the best you can, but don't
try for total mastery. Proceed to the other chapters; then as you encounter
concepts that were introduced in Chapter 1, look them up here. (Like the
other chapters, this one has its own table of contents, but the table doesn't
include much detail. I suggest folding down the corners of some key pages
so that you can turn to them quickly when you need them.) You will find
yourself comprehending both the later chapters and this one better and better
as you move along.*

Jean Piaget* is a Swiss psychologist who was trained in zoology and whose major interests are essentially philosophical. He and his associates have been publishing their findings on the development of cognitive processes in children since 1927, and have accumulated the largest store of factual and theoretical observations extant today.

Piaget and His Methods

Piaget is often criticized because his method of investigation, although somewhat modified in recent years, is still largely clinical. He observes the child's surroundings and his behavior, formulates a hypothesis concerning the structure that underlies and includes them both, and then tests that hypothesis by altering the surroundings slightly—by rearranging the materials, by posing the problem in a different way, or even by overtly suggesting to the subject a response different from the one predicted by the theory.

An example of the method is the investigation of a young child's conception of velocity. The child observes the movement of an object through points *A, B, C,* and *D*. He reports that the object passed through point *D* "after" point *A* and that it took "more time" to get from *A* to *C* than from *A* to *B*. From this it might reasonably be inferred that the child's conception of temporal succession and duration is the same as that of an adult. But the investigation does not stop there. The subject is then presented with the simultaneous movements of

---

*Pronounced *Pyasey:* *ya* as in "yak," *s* as in "pleasure," and *ey* as in "they."

two objects. The investigator systematically varies the actual distance through which each of the objects moves, their times in transit, and their initial and terminal positions relative to one another. When that is done, the child no longer responds as an adult would in similar circumstances. For example, if two objects move simultaneously—that is, if they start simultaneously and stop simultaneously—but at different velocities, the child will deny their simultaneity of movement. To him, each moving object has a different "time"—a time that is a function of the *spatial* features of the display.

The systematic manipulation of variables illustrated by that example is certainly in the tradition of classical experimental science. The example, however, is drawn from one of the more rigorous of the studies done by Piaget and his colleagues. Their investigations often begin with naturalistic observations and continue as an interaction between the child and the "experimenter"— an interaction in which each varies his own behavior in response to that of the other.

Another example may serve to illustrate the point: It is an "experiment" designed to reveal the child's conception of number. The child is presented with an assemblage of coins and a large number of flowers; he is asked to tell how many flowers he can purchase with the coins if the price of each flower is one coin. Here is a transcript of one such encounter:

> Gui (four years, four months) put 5 flowers opposite 6 pennies, then made a one-for-one exchange of 6 pennies for 6 flowers (taking the extra flower from the reserve supply). The pennies were in a row and the flowers bunched together: "What have we done?—*We've exchanged them.*—Then is there the same number of flowers

and pennies?—*No.*—Are there more on one side?—
Yes.—Where?—*There* (pennies). (The exchange was again
made, but this time the pennies were put in a pile and
the flowers in a row.) Is there the same number of flowers
and pennies?—*No.*—Where are there more?—*Here*
(flowers).—And here (pennies)?—*Less.*[1]

This shifting of experimental procedures to fit the responses of a particular subject makes replication difficult, and the results may be especially susceptible to the
"experimenter effect."* Readers who feel impelled to
criticize Piaget's method are in good company. But before becoming too enthusiastically critical, they should
be sure to note the deliberate effort that is made to give
the child opportunities for responses that would *not* fit
the theory or that might suggest extensions of it in un-
expected directions. They should also keep in mind Piaget's epistemological position that knowledge is action
(although not necessarily motor action). The subject is
continually acting. His actions are structured, and they
are also to some extent autonomous. The investigator
must therefore continually change his line of attack if
he is to follow those actions and to discern their under-
lying structure. Indeed, since that structure does differ
from child to child, the investigator may find it necessary
at times to vary his language when posing a problem in
order to ensure that the problem *will* be the same for

---

*Sometimes called the "Rosenthal effect," after R. Rosenthal, who
in several studies demonstrated that, even in apparently objective
experimental situations, the experimenter can influence the subject's
behavior in a number of subtle and unacknowledged ways (facial
expression, tone of voice, and so on). Even rat subjects perform
better for experimenters who expect them to do so, presumably
because of differences in handling by different experimenters.[2]

different children. Rigidly standardized procedures might defeat the very purpose for which they were designed, because their meanings vary from one subject to another. The important thing is to "make contact with the child's thinking."[3]

Relation to American Psychology

The early work of Piaget's Geneva group was given considerable attention in the scholarly press, but, because psychology, especially in the United States, was at that time dominated by associationistic theories of learning and by content-oriented psychometrics, their work generated little interest.

The current explosion of interest in Piaget's work is an expression of the same concern that has produced conceptions of human beings as rule-formulating, rule-following organisms and of their brains as incredibly complex organic systems for processing information. That concern may have resulted not only from a dissatisfaction with existing theories but also from advances that have taken place recently in neurophysiology and computer engineering advances that have not articulated with the theory but have helped to create a favorable climate for it.

In any case, Piaget's observations and formulations are today a definite focus of theoretical and professional interest in psychology. The theory is cognitive. (A cognitive theory is concerned especially with central organizing processes in higher animals, and it recognizes a partial autonomy of those processes, such that the animal becomes an actor on, rather than simply a reactor to, its environment.) It is concerned primarily with structure rather than content—with *how* the mind works rather than with *what* it does. It is concerned more with understanding than with prediction and control of behavior.

These remarks can of course be made only by way of emphasis, for we can never know the *how* except through the *what;* we can only infer central processes from the behaviors that they organize. An affirmation of one kind of analysis does not necessarily imply a negation of the other. There are conflicts between them, but sometimes the dissonance is more apparent than real, and a careful reading of both kinds of analysis reveals a harmony that could not be seen at first glance. In this book, discussion of Piaget's theory is written only partly in the idiom of Piaget. *Input, output,* and *feedback,* for example, are less-than-lyrical words that American psychologists have borrowed from engineering. Piaget generally does without them, but we shall find them useful. Even the term *learning* appears very seldom in Piaget's writings, and when it does, it is nearly always accompanied by a modifier. Conditioning and other specific learnings he calls *learning in the narrow sense;* changes in cognitive structure usually are referred to not as "learning in the broad sense" but as *development,* possibly because of the biological implications of development. In this book, we shall use both the Piagetian and the more standard psychological terms and attempt to understand how they are all related.

One more thing should be said about his system in relation to others. Piaget's early academic training was in zoology, and his theory of cognitive development is rooted firmly there. That, coupled with the feature of invariant stages, has caused some writers to label the theory "nativist," as though it were holding the child's genetic program responsible for the organization of his behavior. But Piaget's is not a nativist theory. A radical alternative to nativism is "empiricism," the doctrine that behavior is determined by the environment—by reinforcement contingencies and the like. But the theory is not empiricist, either. Piaget himself has called it "constructivist": the organism *inherits* a genetic program that gradually (through a process called "maturation") provides the biological equipment necessary for *constructing* a stable internal structure out of its experiences with its *environment.* That stable structure—that "intelligence"— then helps the organism adapt to *changes* in that environment. A paradox? Perhaps, but our discussions of assimilation, accommodation, and equilibration will attempt to resolve it.

Before turning to the first of the Piagetian periods of development, let us take a quick overview of the theory, in preparation for the more detailed account that will follow.

Evolutionary Perspective

The evolution of complex organisms has necessarily been accompanied by that of complex behavioral control systems. A one-celled animal reacts in a severely limited way to its immediate environment; a higher animal has an elaborate repertoire of responses to a wide variety of stimuli. But that elaboration and that flexibility are achieved at the expense of biological simplicity; such an animal is composed of many parts—some specialized for reception of information from the environment, others for actions on it. If it is to adapt successfully to its environment, the higher animal therefore must possess a transmission device that integrates the activities of the parts. And of course if it is to survive, the animal *must* adapt.

But once a transmission system has been established, the way is open to the development of alternative arrangements of that system. Thus, not only are the higher animal's reception and response capabilities complex, but so are the mechanisms that relate those capabilities; relations between stimulus and response are different for higher and lower animals. A lower animal is "sense-dominated"; its response to a specific input from the environment is immediate and preditable. A higher animal's behavior, however, is controlled not only by inputs from its immediate surroundings, but also by mediating processes within the transmission system—processes that are partly the result of previous functioning of the system. Therefore, the higher animal's overt response to a specific input is not necessarily immediate, and it is not predictable merely from knowledge of the current input pattern. To predict the behavior of a higher animal, it is necessary to know something about its mediating processes. In order to predict a human subject's response to a combination of digits—say "8" and "2"— I would have to know what he had learned about arithmetic before he ever came into my laboratory; whether he had in the immediate past been instructed to add, to subtract, to multiply, or to divide; whether he had a generalized set to follow directions; and so on. A person's behavior is determined both by the sensory input at the moment and by the way in which his system of mediating processes has been organized.[4]

The twin consequences of sensory and motor differentiations and of the organization of mediating processes are (1) the extension—both spatially and temporally—of the world with which the organism can interact and (2) the freedom to *choose* from among many possible actions. In this context, "intelligence" is the ability to make adaptive choices.

Structure, Function, and Content

Adaptation is a biological function. As a child develops, *functions* remain invariant, but *structures* change systematically. Change in structures *is* "development."

Another term found often in Piaget's writings is *content*. In an infant, contents are mostly observable stimuli and responses. We may talk in abstract terms about "function" and "structure," but as soon as we cite an actual example, we must deal also with content.

Such an example might be "A baby looks at a rattle and picks it up." The structure of that event relates the means (looking, reaching, grasping) to the end (stimulation from the object in hand). Each of those is related thereby to the other, and it is that relatedness that Piaget calls "structure." The *function* of the baby's act is *adaptation*—that is, the assimilation of input to structure and the accommodation of structure to input. The word *content* refers to the raw data of the action, as distinguished from its pattern, whereas *structure* refers to its systemic properties. In this case, *structure* refers not so much to the actions of looking, reaching, and grasping or to the changing stimuli from eyes, hands, muscles, and joints (the *contents* of the act) as it does to the systematic relations among all of these—relations that must be represented internally even though they are tied securely to external events.*

---

*For more on structure, see the section on "Schemes."

During the course of development, the internal aspect of representation becomes more important and less dependent on external events. As an adult, you look at objects and pick them up, too; but you also think about what you might do next, about the unseen events that caused your car to stall this morning, about Brutus stabbing Caesar and your history professor teetering on the edge of the lecture platform as he tells you about it. There may be wide variations in their clarity and fidelity, but all of these are *contents* of thought. Our concern with contents will be mainly as a means of identifying structures, and the structures that concern us most are the relatively complicated logical and quasi-logical ones that comprise "intelligence" at its best. (Your thoughts about the possible causes of this morning's automotive misfortune probably would be more interesting to Piaget than the others mentioned.)

Finally, *function* refers to biologically inherited modes of interacting with the environment—modes that are characteristic of such integrations in all biological systems. With reference to intelligence, that inherited "functional nucleus" imposes "certain necessary and irreducible conditions"[5] on structures. *Discontinuities* in structure arise out of the *continuous action* of invariant functions. Throughout the developmental period, functions are permanent, but structures are transitory; if they weren't, there would be no development.

There are two basic functions: *adaptation* ("the accord of thought with things"[6]) and *organization* ("the accord of thought with itself"[7]). Adaptation and organization are therefore two aspects of a single mechanism: Adaptation is the external aspect, organization the internal. Organization is the formation of complex structures out of simpler ones; each mental action is a part of an increasingly comprehensive *system* of such actions. Adaptation, in turn, consists of *assimilation* and *accommodation*.

Functional Invariants: Assimilation and Accommodation

If we think of the human brain as an organic machine for processing information, we must realize not only that it is an exceedingly complex machine but also that its internal structure is continually changing. We must realize also that the precise pattern of activity initiated by an incoming stimulus is a function not only of the pattern of the stimulus, but also of the way in which the brain has been programmed to deal with it.

Assimilation occurs whenever an organism uses something from its environment and incorporates it. A biological example would be the ingestion of food. The food is changed in the process, and so is the organism. (Psychological processes are similar in that the pattern in the stimulation is changed, and, again, so is the organism.) When food is eaten, it is transformed in such a way that its nutrients can be transported through the body in the blood. The object is *assimilated* by the digestive system; the changes that occur in it depend on the characteristics of that system—that is, on its *structure*, which is to say on its characteristic *manner of functioning.**
Meanwhile, the system's characteristic manner of func-

---

*Biologists usually use the term *structure* to refer to anatomy rather than to action, as I am using it here.

tioning (its structure) is altered to some extent by the nature of the object that is being ingested—whether it is large or small, hard or soft, acidic or alkaline, and so on. The system *accommodates* to the object; the changes that occur in it depend on the characteristics of the object. The relation of accommodation to assimilation is therefore reciprocal. In psychology, the relation of accommodation to assimilation is also reciprocal: The system is changed by the object, and the object is changed by the system. And these changes occur simultaneously.

For a psychological example, we may look briefly ahead to a section of Chapter 2 that describes the elaboration of means to a desired end in one of Piaget's own children. Fifteen-month-old Jacqueline is in her play pen; an 8-inch stick lies within her reach but outside the bars of the pen, which are about 2½ inches apart. Her problem is to get the stick inside. Jacqueline first grasps the stick near one end but not near enough to enable her to pull that end between two of the bars. When she pulls on it, she merely lodges the stick more firmly against the bars, which are perpendicular to it. She is assimilating the stick to the structure of reaching-grasping-pulling—a structure that has previously accommodated to many different objects in many different situations and hence has become extremely adept at assimilating such objects. In *this* situation, however, this structure that has previously been so effective is inadequate. It must accommodate to the presence of those vertical bars. How that accommodation actually came about is recounted in some detail in Chapter 2. The point to be made here is that, to fulfill their adaptive function, structures must accommodate as well as assimilate.

It may be helpful to think of *two* functions of accom-

modation (though Piaget has not analyzed it in this way).
The first is to make it possible for a particular structure
to operate—that is, to make possible the momentary
assimilation of an event in the environment. The second
function of accommodation is to change the structure
in such a way that it can more easily assimilate similar
events in the future. The reason I suggest this distinction
is that all accommodations perform the first function,
while only some perform the second. It is the second
that most clearly exemplifies "learning in the broad
sense"—that is, intellectual development.

Assimilation and accommodation are called "functional invariants" because they are characteristic of all
biological systems, regardless of the contents of those
systems and the levels at which they function. They are
thus to be contrasted with *structures,* which are the *ways*
in which the systems function. Functions are said to be
invariant because they are present in every act of intelligence, whereas structures vary with the person's stages
of development and with the tasks that confront him
during those stages.

Assimilation and accommodation are always present,
but they are not always in balance one with the other.
Imbalances occur when children are imitating (accommodation over assimilation) and when they are playing
(assimilation over accommodation). Behavior is most
adaptive when accommodation and assimilation are in
balance; but such a balance is always temporary, because
the process of adaptation reveals imperfections in the
system. (See the section on "Equilibration.")

We have been examining one kind of equilibration:
the achievement of a balance between the assimilations
of objects to structures and the accommodation of structures to objects. I chose that kind for our discussion

because in its external aspect it is relatively easy to describe. But there are also equilibrations that are *internal*—some among structures "of the same rank," some between subordinate and superordinate structures.[8] Such internal coordinations are essential to the development of intelligence, and they all involve the *reciprocal assimilation* of structures. Just as every scheme "attempts" to assimilate every object, so do schemes tend to assimilate each other. When an infant reaches, grasps, and sucks, for example, those schemes are coordinated by reciprocal assimilation. Because in any such relationship there are bound to be aspects of one structure that resist assimilation by another, one or both structures must also *accommodate* to that difficulty if the assimilation is to succeed.

Schemes

As I mentioned previously, cognitive development consists of a succession of changes, and the changes are structural.

Piaget often refers to individual structures as *schemes*.* A scheme is an instrument for assimilation. It is a kind of minisystem. It is that property of an action which can be generalized to other contents. For example, the infant who "looks at a *rattle* and picks it up" (p. 11) can do the same with *any* small, lightweight object; the "look-and-pick-up" scheme can assimilate a wide variety of objects—with some accommodations, of course. (The baby must reach farther for distant than for near objects, stretch his fingers more for large than for small objects,

---

*Sometimes called *schemata*, the plural of *schema*, which some authors use as I am using *scheme*.

lift or pull harder for heavy than for light objects, and so on.) Incidentally, to "apply a scheme to an event" is the same as to "assimilate that event to that scheme." We will make use of both phrasings.

So a scheme is the structure of an interaction. In our example, the interaction is between the scheme and an external object. But there are also interactions among schemes; they can assimilate each other and accommodate to each other. The tendency to combine lower-order structures into coherent systems is called *organization*. Actually, because each structure is itself a system, organization is the tendency to develop ever more comprehensive systems (higher-order structures).

A scheme is a unit of structure; "whatever is repeatable or generalizable" is a scheme.[9] The earliest structures are relatively simple; they are often referred to as *reflexes*. Later, largely as a result of reciprocal assimilation and accommodation, schemes are more complex—more "mental"—and it becomes increasingly appropriate to think of them as "coordinations," "strategies," "plans," "transformation rules," "expectancies," and so on. Whatever their labels, they form a kind of framework onto which incoming sensory data can fit—indeed must fit if they are to have any effect; but it is a framework that is continually changing its shape so that as many data as possible *will* fit.

Figure 1.1 summarizes some of these relationships.

Relations Among Structures and Functions

Figure 1.1 is an attempt to represent the relationships among *function, organization, adaptation, accommodation, assimilation, structure,* and *scheme.* It will not be a suc-

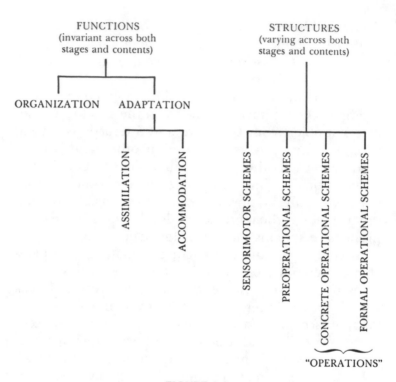

FIGURE 1.1

cessful attempt, however, if the diagram is conceived as an ordinary classification hierarchy in which, at any given level, each category is a viable entity unto itself. Having divided a deck of cards into spades, hearts, diamonds, and clubs, you can throw away all the hearts, say, or all the clubs, without affecting the contents of the remaining categories; those categories still exist, and in the same form as before. But without *functions,* there can *be* no structures, and vice versa; without *assimilation,* there can be no *accommodation,* and vice versa; and *accommodation* is a change in *structure,* the function of which is to make possible the *assimilation* of some stimulus pattern that is not entirely familiar. Similarly, unless *adaptation* is *organized,* it is not adaptive. Furthermore, the *structures* that in the diagram are separate from *functions* are really *ways of functioning*—the enduring results of organizing adaptation (or adaptive organizing).

This attempt at extensive qualification of the apparently simple relations depicted in Figure 1.1 may be confusing, but it should serve to emphasize one of the salient features of Piaget's theory: Everything is related to everything else. The various entities in the diagram actually represent different aspects of a single entity: a functioning cognitive system.

Figurative and Operative Aspects of Thought

Piaget's is a "cognitive" theory (see definition on p. 7), so he shares with other cognitive psychologists a concern for central organizing processes in general and for thinking in particular. But his theory is also different from theirs. One feature that sets Piaget's theory apart is his distinction between the figurative and the operative aspects of thinking.

Like other cognitive theorists, Piaget places great emphasis on internal representations of external events. For him, however, there are two kinds of representation: representation in the narrow sense and representation in the broad sense. He sees in the other theories only representation in the narrow sense. Other theorists use words, images, "fractional stimuli," and so on, to represent internally that which before learning had been external. A word, for example, literally represents a particular external event or class of events, and according to those theorists the structure of interactions among internalized words and other symbols constitutes an individual's intelligence.

So far, so good, says Piaget, except that thinking is not, as the others claim, merely a systematic interaction of direct representations of external reality; that is representation in the narrow sense. Representation in the broad sense is the whole of knowing activity, and it involves not just an interaction but a *transformation* of input patterns. For Piaget, the direct internal representation of external reality is but one aspect of thought—the *figurative* aspect. The transformation is referred to as the *operative* aspect. (To operate is to act; the organism acts on the input to construct a known object. It would not be far wrong to call this aspect "action knowledge.")

All of this might remain incomprehensible if you were not already acquainted with the notions of accommodation and assimilation. Given that acquaintance, it should be easy; for direct representation comes about through accommodation, and transformation occurs by assimilation. When a small child encounters a wooden block, for example, he adjusts the structure of his action to it: He stretches his body and arm far enough to reach it, stretches his thumb and fingers far enough to encompass it, he clamps down on it, he exerts enough upward force to lift it, and so on. In other words, he *accommodates* to the object. When that accommodation becomes internalized, it serves as a direct representation of the object itself. It is the *figurative* aspect of the representation. "Whenever in an act of knowing the accommodative activity is oriented toward the organization of sensory data, Piaget refers to that aspect of knowing as 'figurative' "[10]*

But accommodation cannot occur unless there is a structure to accommodate; so, while it is accommodating, the structure is also assimilating; and, as I mentioned earlier, assimilation is a *transforming* process. In the preceding example, there *is* a figurative aspect to the child's representation of the wooden block, but it is not the critical feature of his knowledge of the block. If the child has placed this block on top of another, for example, or if he has used it as a support for some other object, the schemes to which the block is assimilated may include one or the other of those activities—or possibly even a higher-order scheme that coordinates the two (a "stacking scheme"?). Or he may note the similarity of the block's physical configuration to that of a truck and thence assimilate it to a truck scheme. In other words, assimilation to those schemes gives the block its *meaning;* it is the *operative* aspect of knowing. Representation in the broad sense (knowing) includes meaning, and meaning is operative.

To summarize: Any knowing activity is *representation in the broad sense.* As such, it always includes both assimilation and accommodation Assimilation is the principal component of the *operative* aspect of knowing; and, if

---

*Notice that this is virtually the opposite of *figurative* as it appears in common speech. If you say "figuratively speaking," you mean that what you are saying is *not* to be taken as actual, objective, or literally true. But that is exactly what it does mean in the quotation above. In this usage, it refers to the bare physical configurations of an event as distinguished from its possible meanings. The term *figurative* is the mental counterpart of the *figural* aspect of the physical environment.

it is oriented toward the organization of sensory data (as distinguished from internal structures), the knowing also has an accommodation-dominated *figurative* aspect, which Piaget regards as *representation in the narrow sense.*

There is another term that is figurally very similar to "operative" (it looks and sounds like it) but has a rather different meaning. Schemes are "operative" throughout a person's life, but at a certain stage of his development they become also "operational." Sensorimotor schemes are operative but not operational; operational schemes are both. "Operational," then, means "operative at a particular level of development"—a level about which you will soon be learning a great deal. Just be careful not to confuse the two terms on the basis of their figural similarity.

Relations Between Figurative and Operative Aspects of Thought: "Memory" as an Example

Most people think of memory in terms of stored copies of past sensory impressions. But that is an *empiricist* view (that the only source of knowledge is experience), and Piaget will have none of it. For him, memory involves an active *construction* at the time of exposure and an equally active reconstruction at the time of recall. (Our discussion will be confined to the type of memory that Piaget calls "evocation" of an image memory and that nearly everyone else calls "recall.")

Three Kinds of Figurative Representation

Not that experience is not important. Obviously, if there is a representation of the past, there must have been some accommodation to patterns of sensory input in the past. Piaget has classified such accommodations under three headings: "perception," "imitation," and "image." *Perception* is a constructive activity as opposed to a passive reception, to be sure, but it is sharply focused on present patterns of sensory input, as in seeing, hearing, and touching. (In Chapter 2, you will have an opportunity to see perception develop.) Perception implies memory only to the extent that its assimilative schemes are the result of previous activity. *Imitation* is a motor activity the goal of which is to mimic the structure of the environment, as in reproducing the contours of an object (such as a ball) or the actions of an adult (such as waving "bye-bye") by a motion of the hands. (You will find many references to imitation in Chapters 2 and 3.) Some imitations (called "deferred" imitations) occur in the absence of the model and hence imply memory. (Again, see Chapters 2 and 3.) An *image* is an internalized imitation. It has an important role to play in the development of symbols (a development we shall discuss in Chapter 3). Because images are independent of current input, they, too, imply memory. Most of the present discussion will pertain to image as the figural aspect of memory.

Two Kinds of Memory

Just as Piaget has made a distinction between "learning in the narrow sense" on the one hand and "development" (not "learning in the broad sense") on the other, so he has also distinguished between "memory in the specific sense" and "conservation of schemes" (not "memory in the broad sense").

The term *memory in the specific sense* refers to the *figurative* aspect of remembering. It is concerned with specific objects or events, such as your history professor teetering on the edge of a speaker's platform or your automobile standing motionless in the middle of a busy intersection. The image is localized in both time and space. It is almost like a perception in the absence of adequate stimuli, because it is in fact derived from previous accommodation to those stimuli. In short, it is an *image*. The term *conservation of schemes* refers to the *operative* aspect of memory. It is the continuity of general ways of functioning, such as driving your car or figuring out "What's the matter with it *this* time?" The schemes are timeless and not localized in space; you can apply them, with some accommodations of course, to different cars and various malfunctions. Their work may often be manifested in specific images, but specific images are not necessary parts of the schemes. This aspect of memory is coexistent with intelligence itself—that is, with the operativity of schemes. To put it another way, the memory of a scheme *is* that scheme; the very existence of a scheme implies its conservation.

If this seems a bit foggy at the moment, return to it after reading the next section. It contains an illustration that should clarify what must seem a very strange conception of memory.

An Illustrative Experiment

If I hand you ten wooden rods and ask you to arrange them in order of size, you seek out the smallest of the lot first, then the next-to-smallest, and so on until the series is complete. If at any time you discover that you have overlooked a rod, you can insert it later with no difficulty whatever.

Not so with younger subjects. Piaget has tested many children at varying stages of development, and he has found that their performances progress through four stages:

Stage I
The youngest children do not "seriate" at all.

Stage II
Later, there is seriation all right, but it is based entirely on the alignment of the tops of the rods; the bottoms are allowed to vary at random.*

Stage III
Still later, children can arrange correctly although haltingly the original elements of the series; but they are baffled if presented with new ones to be inserted at various places. They do not know where those places are and usually prefer to reconstruct the entire series.

Stage IV
Finally, subjects achieve "operational seriation" in which they begin at one end of the series and promptly arrange all the original rods correctly, then insert extra ones into their proper places as required.

So far I have not said anything about memory, or for that matter about the figurative and operative aspects of thought that it is supposed to illustrate. The reason is that Piaget has a hypothesis that what is remembered depends on the subject's stage of intellectual develop-

---

*Actually, Stage II is further analyzed into five substages. The one depicted here is the middle one of those substages.[11]

ment. Now that we have seen the stages illustrated in the simple seriation problem, we are in a position to test that hypothesis. Our experiment goes something like this:[12]

First Session

1a. The subject is shown a previously constructed series that is correct and complete.

1b. He is asked to look at it carefully and remember it.

Second Session (a week after the first)

2a. The subject is asked to demonstrate what he remembers: he traces the configuration on a table with his fingers and he draws a picture of it on paper.

2b. His developmental level is tested immediately by allowing him to arrange the rods himself and by introducing additional elements as described earlier under Stages III and IV.

2c. His drawing ability is tested by presenting him with a completed series and asking him to draw it with the model present.

Third Session (eight months after the first)

3a. Same as 2a.

3b. Same as 2b.

3c. Same as 3b.

As I mentioned earlier, Piaget believes that recall memory, far from being a static copy of previous impressions, involves an active construction at the time of exposure and a reconstruction at the time of recall. If he is right, each subject's performance at any given time should be a function of his intellectual level, not just at the time of exposure, but also at the time of recall. It is, after all, his "intelligence" that is doing both the construction and the reconstruction.

The results tend to confirm this view. The more advanced the subject's developmental stage at the time of exposure and first test of memory (they were separated by only a week), the more accurately he remembered the configuration. That much might be predicted by a sophisticated empiricist theory on the ground that with more experience behind him the more advanced subject has a more sophisticated system of information reception, storage, and retrieval than that of the younger child. What is astonishing, however, is that, when a subject's developmental level *changes* between tests, memory changes right along with it! For example, suppose a child's developmental level (tested at 2b) is at Stage II and his drawing (2c) is one good copy of the model. Suppose, further, that at the time of the first test the child is on the verge of passing into Stage III. Then his second memory test (3a) will show not the decrement that you might expect over several months' time but an actual *improvement* to correspond to his new developmental level!

Piaget is not at all astonished by this result, because it conforms to his theory. According to his analysis, the figuratively oriented image of the rods is in every instance assimilated to the operative schemes of that moment—that is, to the child's intelligence. What the subject draws is therefore not a copy of what he has seen in the past; rather, it is a rendition of what he knows now. If the model is *present* during the drawing, any discrepancies between the figure (the series of rods) and his interpretation of it become immediately apparent, and he resolves them in favor of the figure. (Of course, some of the younger subjects cannot even do that.) But when the figure is *not* present, the drawing reflects his own construction, and, as his intelligence improves, so does his drawing.

Come to think of it, maybe we should not be so shocked by that result, which is a straightforward implication of Piaget's dictum that all knowledge is constructed. If I ask you to recall getting dressed this morning, the resultant memory will have a definite figural content, but that content is only one aspect of a *construction*. The socks go on before the shoes not because you have a movie projector in your head but because you *know* that socks go on before shoes, so you reconstruct the event in that way. At every level of intelligence, figurative knowledge has its operative aspects. At the higher levels, the figurative aspect becomes differentiated from and directed by operative intelligence. At every level, memories are *constructed*.

Equilibration

One concept that is not represented by the diagram in Figure 1.1 is that of *equilibration*. The word will not be used often in this book, but the idea to which it refers should be kept constantly in mind while studying Piaget's theory in subsequent chapters, for it was the inspiration for the theory in the first place and remains its overarching principle.

Equilibration is a function of every living system. It is a process of attaining equilibrium between external intrusions and the activities of the organism. From a psychological point of view, those activities may be conceived as strategies for maximizing gains of information and minimizing losses.[13] Equilibration is a mechanism of change that operates over an extended period of time in a developing child. To place it in proper perspective, it should be compared to another such mechanism: *learning*.

Behaviorists think of learning as the formation of associations. A response occurs in the presence of a stimulus, and a bond is formed such that henceforth when that stimulus is presented, that response will occur. Often there is an added requirement that the response be followed immediately by a special kind of stimulus called a *reinforcer*.

Although Piaget does not deny that such learning occurs, he has concluded that the fundamental process in learning is not association. He calls association "learning in the narrow sense," and is not much interested in it. What does interest him is a complex that includes maturation and a different kind of learning—a complex that he calls "development."

Possibly the most important difference between Piaget's developmental theory and traditional learning theory is that in addition to the gradual *accretion of functional associations* (isolated simple structures), Piaget's theory recognizes an intermittent *revision of established structures*—a process that entails qualitative as well as quantitative change as higher-order structures (schemes) incorporate those of an earlier stage. The process by which structures are revised is called equilibration.

Equilibration is "coming into equilibrium." In classical physics, there are two kinds of equilibrium: *static* and *dynamic*. A balance scale with equal weights in the two pans is a system in static equilibrium, as indeed is any body at rest. In contrast, a thermostat is in dynamic equilibrium; so is a homeostatic biological system, a falling body after its acceleration has ceased, or any other system in which an interchange of forces maintains the system in a constant state. In Piaget's theory, equilibrium is dynamic; it is a system of compensating actions that maintain a steady state. That steady state is a condition of the system in which the internal activities of the organism completely compensate for intrusions from without. Because of the importance of states (stages) in his theory, Piaget has often seemed uninterested in mechanisms of transition from one state to another; but the concept of equilibration is concerned with just those transitions.

An example is the acquisition of *conservation of continuous quantity*. See Figure 1.2. The subject is presented with two identical beakers that have been filled to exactly the same level with fruit juice; one is identified as his, the other as the experimenter's. After the child has acknowledged that the amount of juice is the same in each jar, the experimenter pours the contents of one jar into a short, broad container and that of the other into a tall, thin one. "Now," he says to the child, "Do you have

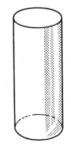

CONTAINER *A*   CONTAINER *B*

FIGURE 1.2

more to drink, or do I, or do we have the same amount?" If the answer is "same amount," the subject is said to have "conserved" the substance of the liquid. With respect to this problem, at least, his thinking is "equilibrated."

According to Piaget, this, like all equilibration processes, goes through four steps.[14] In Step 1, the subject attends to only one dimension (usually the height), and he judges the tall drink to be the larger; he fails to "conserve" quantity. Repeated experiences with configurations that are similar but not identical, however (liquids poured into vessels of varying shapes, from vessel to vessel, and so on), eventually lead him to shift to the other dimension (in this case width). That shift is especially likely when the tall drink is constricted into a mere tube, for then its extreme thinness can hardly escape his attention, and he does indeed state that the tall drink is now the *smaller* of the two. "Focusing on the other dimension" is the second of the four steps of equilibration. The third step is a mixture of the first two—or rather, it is an alternation between them as the conditions of the display are changed. But that alternation, especially if it is rapid, provides the necessary condition of the fourth step, which is simultaneous attention to both height and width and their coordination into a mutually compensating system. *Now* when he is asked, "Which has more to drink?" he replies firmly, "They are the same." Notice that the outcome of all this is not a copy of external reality, but a way of dealing with it more effectively.

A child approaches any conservation problem with a strategy for obtaining information from it. But the more consistently he applies that strategy (Step 1), the clearer it becomes to him that it is inadequate; so he shifts to another strategy (Step 2). When the second strategy also fails, he vacillates between the first two (Step 3), which results eventually in a stable system (Step 4) that modifies each and includes both. Now he has information not only about changes in one dimension (such as the height of a body of liquid) or about changes in another (such as its width), but about both of those plus conservation of whatever remains the same (such as the quantity of the liquid) throughout all those changes. The last strategy will not itself disintegrate; but it does contribute to further change, for its very stability makes possible an awareness of inadequacies in larger systems of which it becomes a part.

Structures continually move toward equilibrium, and when a state of relative equilibrium has been attained, a scheme is sharper, more clearly delineated, than it had been previously. But the very sharpness points up inconsistencies and gaps in the structure that had never been salient before. Each equilibrium state therefore carries with it the seeds of its own destruction, for the child's activities are thenceforth directed toward reducing those inconsistencies and closing those gaps. Equilibrium is always dynamic and is never absolute, but the product of each of the major units of development (Sensorimotor, Concrete Operations, and Formal Operations) is a relatively equilibrated system of actions—an *equilibrium* (equilibrated structure).

Equilibration as Motivation

Piaget has acknowledged the distinction between learning and intelligence, on the one hand, and emotion and motivation, on the other, and he has chosen to deal explicitly and at length with the former but not with the latter. Implicitly, however, his theory of intellectual development does include a motivational component. The brain as a biological organ is active, and in the normal course of events its activity becomes structured. Once a structure (scheme) has been formed, it spontaneously assimilates whatever it can; thinking does not need to be "reinforced." Or, to put it another way, the reinforcement is inherent within the thinking itself. "Each scheme provides its own need to be fed and to act. The scheme starts to reproduce, to repeat itself and to incorporate all sorts of new things into itself."[15] And, of course, as the scheme assimilates it also accommodates; so learning is motivated from within the thinking-learning system— that is, within intelligence.

This is not to say that learning cannot be motivated from without. It can, but Piagetian educators are suspicious of "gimmicks" designed to motivate children to learn. They regard learning as an integral component of equilibration, and equilibration occurs spontaneously.

Development and Learning

Intelligence can be conceived as either a cause or an effect of learning. On p. 8, I pointed out that Piaget distinguishes "development" from "learning in the narrow sense." Development "concerns the totality of the structure of knowledge"[16]—that is, it concerns intelligence. (This section could just as well have been labeled "Intelligence and Learning.") Learning (in the narrow sense), however, "is a limited process—limited to a single problem, or to a single structure."[17]

Because development occurs spontaneously, whereas

learning must be "provoked,"[18] Piaget comes down hard on one side of the question posed by the first sentence of this section: Intelligence is a *cause* of learning and not, as most American psychologists would say, its effect. The difference between him and them is not as sharp as it may appear, however, for the "spontaneous" development of mental structures is not simply the playing out of a genetic program; it requires continual nourishment from a wide variety of *experiences,* as you will see in the following section.

Factors in Development

Equilibration is not the only factor in the intellectual development of a child (although it is the most important). Altogether, there are five:* maturation, physical experience, logico-mathematical experience, social transmission, and equilibration.

Maturation

To some psychologists, *maturation* is simply (?) the process of attaining maturity, whatever the nature of that process might be. Piaget uses the term more specifically to refer to a gradually unfolding genetic plan. Genetic effects are never seen in isolation, of course; but it does

---

*The categories "physical experience" and "logico-mathematical experience" are often reduced to subcategories under the single category "experience."[19] That does not appeal to me because "social transmission" is also experience, but is not included in the category.

seem worthwhile to abstract them from the flux or life for purposes of analysis. In any case, that is what Piaget has done, and in his writing maturation refers to genetic influences on development.

Physical Experience

Interacting with the genetic effects is a factor called *physical experience,* which the child uses to abstract the various properties of physical objects. Whenever a child squeezes an object and finds it solid, drops it and discovers that it breaks, places it in water and watches it float, or has any other commerce with the object as object, he engages in an abstraction process (*simple* or *empirical* abstraction) that results in knowledge of that particular object and, ultimately, of the material of which the object is constituted. The experience is called *physical* to distinguish it from logico-mathematical experience, but paradoxically it always involves assimilation to logico-mathematical structures. The knowledge that a particular contour is horizontal, for example, depends on the prior construction of a system of spatial coordinates. "Comparing two weights presupposes the establishment of a relation, and therefore the construction of a logical form."[20] Even the knowledge that a single object is "light" or "heavy" entails a comparison with some internalized standard and, again, presupposes the construction of a logical form. So does identifying an object as "wood" or "iron." Even the knowledge that there *is* an "object" requires the coordination of countless actions on particular objects—coordinations that in themselves constitute another kind of experience.

Logico-Mathematical Experience

It is in the nature of things for a child to act on the objects in his environment. When he does so, they "act back," so to speak, and the result is physical experience. But there is another kind of experience that comes when he constructs *relationships* among objects—or rather, among his actions on objects. Piaget relates a story told to him by a mathematician friend, who, at the age of four or five years,

> . . . was seated on the ground in his garden and he was counting pebbles. Now to count these pebbles he put them in a row and he counted them one, two, three, up to ten. Then he finished counting them and started to count them in the other direction. He began by the end and once again he found ten. . . . There were ten in one direction and ten in the other direction. So he put them in a circle and counted them that way and found ten once again.[21]

What that child "learned" (in the broad sense) had to do not with the physical properties of the pebbles but with the relations among them. More precisely, what he accomplished was an organization of his actions with respect to the pebbles.

The concept of "ten"—and the quality of "tenness"—is not a property of pebbles but a construction of the child's mind. The *experience* of that construction, and of others similar to it, is called *logico-mathematical* to distinguish it from physical experience; the process of construction is often called *formal* or *reflective abstraction* because it enables the mind to reflect on the general (and generalizable) form of its own actions.

Social Transmission

The knowledge that a child acquires from physical experience is abstracted from physical objects. In the case of logico-mathematical experience, knowledge is constructed from actions on objects. In social transmission, it comes from other people. They demonstrate, deliberately or otherwise, how things are done; they write things down in books, but mostly they just talk.

And some of their knowledge is acquired by the child. Acquisition of knowledge from another person is said to have occurred via *social transmission.*

In its figurative aspects (the perception, imitation, and imagining of words, gestures, facial expression, huggings, spankings, and so on), social transmission is similar to physical knowledge; but, also like physical knowledge, it always involves assimilation to logico-mathematical structures. Adults who attempt to transmit knowledge to children by "telling" them should be prepared to see their messages assimilated into structures that are very different from their own. The "social transmission" of knowledge is not as easy as it seems.

Equilibration

Last, but definitely not least, is *equilibration,* which integrates the other four factors into itself. In fact, it is so much a part of them (and they of it) that I personally find it difficult to conceive of equilibration as a factor separate from the others. Whenever we talk about the adaptive functions of assimilation and accommodation, for example, we are talking also about equilibration, because it is through their coordination (equilibration) that the functions become adaptive. Every event in the environment must fit into an established operative framework, but at the same time its figural features must be taken into account; it is the equilibrium of these two functions that makes adaptive behavior possible. The special importance of equilibration is implicit in the special treatment given to it in the previous section.

A Theme for the Theory

You will recall that in a section of this chapter entitled "Evolutionary Perspective," I said that, from a psychological point of view, the evolution of human beings has been from sense-dominated automatons to autonomous decision makers. I now suggest that the development of a human *individual* proceeds along that same dimension. At each level, the individual's knowledge of an environmental event consists of the schemes to which that event can be assimilated; but the later schemes are very different from the earlier ones.

In the beginning is the reflex. Piaget's label for the first postnatal month or so of an infant's psychological life is "Exercising the Ready-Made Sensorimotor Schemes." That stage is distinguished by a very simple, dependable relation between input and output. There is an operative aspect of knowing (assimilation to the motor pattern) even here; but because it is almost perfectly correlated with the figurative aspect (accommodation to the sensory pattern), the infant's knowledge, such as it is, reflects that figurative aspect. The function of a scheme at any level is presumably to organize a possible response. But later on schemes will significantly *transform* sensory data, whereas the earliest schemes merely organize immediate responses to the data as given. In that sense, to the extent that he responds at all, the behavior of the neonate is controlled by his present environment.

At the other end of the scale—opposite the sense-dominated automaton—is the intelligent adult. Much of the behavior of an adult is also sense dominated: He walks about, sits down, ties his shoes, drives his car, and so on, mostly "without giving it any thought." In an appropriate figure of speech, he is "on autopilot." But those "automatic" activities are in the service of decisions made previously. Different reactions to the immediate environment *can* be selected. Indeed, an adult at the highest level of intellectual development can *transform* patterns of environmental input to such an extent that for him "reality is only a subset within a much larger set of possibilities" (p. 160 of this book). The implications of this for autonomous decision making are substantial.

Between birth and adulthood, there are many changes in the relation of a person to his environment. Because Piaget emphasizes the qualitative differences of one stage from another, it might be helpful to keep in mind also that intellectual development is a *progression* of stages—that each new stage is closer than its predecessor to a predetermined end. I am suggesting that this progression begins with schemes that organize overt reactions to the *immediate sensory environment* and continues through schemes that are capable of extensive *transformation* of sensory information for particular purposes. I am suggesting, further, that this progression ultimately endows the intelligent adult with a degree of autonomy that would not otherwise be possible.

The progression, then, is from schemes that generate immediate, specific responses in specific situations (such as reflexes) to those that generalize broadly across many situations (such as problem-solving strategies). It is from a world in which self and object are the same to one in which the child sees himself as an object among other objects—a world extended in both time and space. It is from figurative dominance to operative dominance. The quality (as distinguished from quantity) of figurative "representation in the narrow sense" changes very little after infancy. (Adult perception and imagery still consists of objects in space.) So it is important for development that the operative aspect of knowing be differentiated from the figurative—that schemes become increasingly independent of specific content. (Thinking is not limited to present objects in their current configurations.) As the operative aspect gains its independence, the dependence of the figurative becomes increasingly apparent. Operativity dominates, and operative knowing (intelligence) passes through a sequence of "stages" or "periods" of development.

Consolidation of Concepts:
A Working Vocabulary for Beginners

In common speech, many terms function as synonyms. In a mature science, each term has a meaning that is both precise and unique. Psychology's use of terms falls somewhere in between. In conversation, even a single theorist will often use different terms to represent essentially the same idea. Unless the theorist is careful to avoid it, those rather casual references will appear in his writings. Piaget has not been careful. Rather than retrace his steps looking for misplaced terms, he has pressed ever onward, leaving others to follow if they can.

That is tough on you, because it makes a difficult

theory seem even more so. But I believe I can cut the problem down to manageable proportions by indicating the ways in which many of Piaget's terms relate to each other. Table 1.1 is an attempt to do that.

The *figurative* aspect of knowing comes from *physical* experience and provides the manifest *content* of actions. Physical experience in turn consists of *accommodation* to objects. In all of this, orientation is toward the external environment, even when—as occurs more and more frequently with increasing maturity—the actions themselves are internalized.

TABLE 1.1

CONSOLIDATION OF CONCEPTS

External Orientation		*Internal Orientation*	
Figurative Physical Accommodative	} Aspect of Knowing	Operative Logico-Mathematical Assimilative	} Aspect of Knowing
Perception Imitation Image	} Content	Sensorimotor Schemes Preoperational Schemes Concrete Operational Schemes Formal Operational Schemes	} Structure (Form)
Knowledge in the Narrow Sense			
Knowledge in the Broad Sense			

The *operative* or *logico-mathematical* aspect of knowing, however, has to do with the way in which *assimilation* occurs—the *form* that the action takes or the *structure* that is manifested in it. This is the internal, organizing aspect of knowing.

Perception, imitation, and image are *not* interchangeable; nor are the four levels of structure. Indeed, there frequently are reasons for discriminating also among the other terms in Table 1.1. For example, "content" and "structure" are nouns, whereas the remaining six are adjectives. But in general, the content of thought is figurative, physical, or accommodative, whereas its form (structure) is operative, logico-mathematical, or assimilative. For our purposes, "figurative," "physical," and "accommodative" may be considered synonyms, as may "operative," "logico-mathematical," and "assimilative," The other terms are closely related to those two groups, as indicated earlier.

So there is not such a bewildering array of concepts after all. The concepts to which the terms refer are difficult, to be sure, but it should be comforting to know that many of the most important terms can be contained within just four closely related categories:

1. *Externally oriented aspects of knowing* include
2. *contents.*
3. *Internally oriented aspects of knowing* include
4. *structures.*

This consolidation of concepts goes beyond any that Piaget himself has proposed, and although some Piagetian scholars have endorsed it, others may be reluctant to do so. For example, Constance Kamii (personal communication, October 7, 1979) has objected to the identification of accommodation with physical knowing and assimilation with logico-mathematical knowing.

> Whether there is more assimilation than accommodation in any given situation depends not on the type of knowledge involved but on the familiarity of the object and the level of development of the subject.

My position is not that the physical/logico-mathematical ratio *determines* the accommodation/assimilation ratio, but that the physical/logico-mathematical distinction refers to ever-present aspects of knowing, that the accommodative-assimilative distinction also refers to aspects of knowing, and that the two distinctions tend to be drawn in the same situations for the same purposes; that is, they often function as synonyms.

As for familiarity of object and developmental level of subject, I fully agree that they are potent determiners of "whether there is more assimilation than accommodation in any given situation," although the relationship is not a simple one. In general, *the subject who has the best-developed cognitive structure appropriate to a given situation will assimilate most in that situation.* However, that effect on assimilation may not raise the ratio of assimilation to accommodation, for they tend to advance together. When an experienced mechanic looks under the hood of an automobile, he not only assimilates that display in a different way than would a small child or even an average adult; he also accommodates to many objects that to many other people are not objects at all. What *they* see is a single mass of machinery.

However, the learning (changing of structure) function of accommodation does not occur unless there is something in the display that can be assimilated only with some difficulty—something that momentarily *dis-*

equilibrates the system. There has to be a discrepancy between (1) the cognitive structure that is needed to assimilate smoothly and (2) the structure that is available. But the discrepancy must be a relatively small one, else the assimilation may not occur at all. If our mechanic is looking at an engine that features an innovative fuel-mixing device, he can learn something that you or I probably could not because, again, for us the engine is just a mass of machinery. For us, the fuel-mixing device may not even exist.

Among infants and young children, two special kinds of relationship between accommodation and assimilation occur: In imitation, accommodation is dominant, and in play assimilation is dominant. Both are discussed in Chapter 2, where you will find that the external and internal orientations of knowing are represented usually by accommodation and assimilation, occasionally by the figurative-operative distinction. In later chapters, distinctions also will be made among the various levels of structure.

Developmental Levels

Piaget conceives of intellectual development as a continual process of organization and reorganization of structures, each new organization integrating the previous one into itself. Although that process is continuous, its results are discontinuous; they are qualitatively different from time to time. Because of that, Piaget has chosen to break the total course of development into units called *periods* and *stages* (see Table 1.2). Note carefully, however, that each of those cross sections of development is de-

TABLE 1.2

UNITS IN THE DEVELOPMENT OF INTELLIGENCE ACCORDING TO PIAGET

Sensorimotor Period—six stages	
Exercising the ready-made sensorimotor schemes	0-1 mo.
Primary circular reactions	1-4 mo.
Secondary circular reactions	4-8 mo.
Coordination of secondary schemes	8-12 mo.
Tertiary circular reactions	12-18 mo.
Invention of new means through mental combinations	18-24 mo.
Preoperational Period	2-7 yr.
Concrete Operations Period	7-11 yr.
Formal Operations Period	11-15 yr.

More refined versions of this table have been devised, and its terms have different meanings in different contexts. The use of the term *stage*, for example, is not restricted to the marking off of subunits within the Sensorimotor Period. In the generic sense, it may appear in such expressions as "stage theory" or "moving from one stage of development to another," and it is even used *systematically* in ways that differ from its use in Table 1.2. In one of those uses, the Preoperational Period is called "Stage I"; Concrete Operations, "Stage II"; and Formal Operations, "Stage III." In another, Stage I is early Preoperational, Stage II is late Preoperational, and Stage III is both Concrete and Formal Operational. Thus, even when *stage* is used systematically, that usage may be confined to a particular discussion. Henceforth, I shall use the term only in the generic sense.

There is some justification for classifying "Preoperational" as a subperiod under the Concrete Operations Period. But current usage is overwhelmingly otherwise, and the newer terms are easier to use. (The term "Preoperational Subperiod of the Concrete Operations Period" is awkward, to say the least; and "Concrete Operational Subperiod of the Concrete Operations Period" is even more so.)

All age ranges are approximations. Among children in any range, one can usually find manifestations of more than one stage or period. Even the approximations are far from universal: I have seen many references to sensorimotor stages that differ from those in Table 1.1 (some by as much as two months), to 1½ years as the beginning of the Preoperational Period, to "7–8" as the beginning of the Concrete Operational Period, and to "11–12" for that of Formal Operations. There is even some evidence that the final stage is *never* attained by many people. The important point is that the *sequence* of development is the same for everyone.

scribed in terms of the *best* the child can do at that time. Many previously acquired behaviors will occur even though he is capable of new and better ones.

Summary

You have in this chapter the theoretical tools with which to tie all of its parts together. But a tool is not a tool unless you can use it, so at this point you are probably feeling rather helpless. You will gain confidence, as you work your way through the rest of the book, if you will make frequent references to appropriate parts of this chapter. Keep in mind that cognitive development is a process of continual equilibration, and see if you don't agree with my "Theme for the Theory." After you have examined the stages in some detail and you return to review this chapter in its entirety, you will find it infinitely more comprehensible than it is now.

Let's move on to Chapter 2.

Notes

1. Piaget, *The Child's Conception of Number* (1941 [1952]), p. 57.

2. Rosenthal and Fade, "The Effect of Experimenter Bias on the Performance of the Albino Rat" (1963), and Rosenthal and Lawson, " A Longitudinal Study of Experimenter Bias on the Operant Learning of Laboratory Rats" (1964). An interesting study of the experimenter effect in humans is Rosenthal and Jacobson's *Pygmalion in the Classroom* (1968).

3. Duckworth, "Language and Thought" (1973),P. 149.

4. My discussion has been significantly influenced by Hebb's analysis in his *The Organization of Behavior* (1949) and his *A Textbook of Psychology* (1958 [1966]).

5. Piaget, *The Origins of Intelligence in Children* (1936 [1952]), p. 3.

6. *Ibid.*, p. 8.

7. *Ibid.*

8. Piaget, *The Development of Thought: Equilibration of Cognitive Structures (1975 [1977]), p. 40.*

9. Piaget, *Genetic Epistemology (1970), p. 5.*

10. Furth, *Piaget and Knowledge* (1969), p. 135.

11. Piaget and Inhelder, *Memory and Intelligence* (1968 [1972]), p. 29.

12. *Ibid.*, pp. 34–35.

13. Piaget, *Six Psychological Studies* (1964 [1967]), p. 109.

14. Adapted from Flavell's account in his *The Developmental Psychology of Jean Piaget* (1963), pp. 215–249.

15. Piaget, "Problems of Equilibration" (1972), p. 31.

16. Piaget, "Development and Learning" (1964), p. 176.

17. *Ibid.*

18. *Ibid.*

19. Piaget and Inhelder, *The Psychology of the Child* (1966 [1969]), pp. 155–156.

20. *Ibid.*, p. 155.

21. Piaget, "Development and Learning" (1964).

2

The Sensorimotor
Period (0–2 Years)

2

The Sensorimotor
Period (0–2 Years)

As we have seen (Table 1.2), Piaget has divided the Sensorimotor Period into six subperiods that he calls "stages." That much detail is not appropriate in a book of this kind, so we will not concern ourselves with the substages. Instead, we will analyze the period in terms of what I regard as its most important accomplishments.

Object Permanence, Space, and Time

You and I assume that we live in a world of objects, that we apprehend that world as it is, and that's all there is to it! We believe thus because we "know" those objects. But knowing is not as simple as it might seem. To know an object is not merely to register a copy of reality (its figurative aspect) but to *transform* it through assimilation

51

to operative structures. Actually, many of our most rudimentary perceptions are achieved only after much experience.

The inference that an object has *permanence* beyond our immediate perception of it comes even later, for the child must construct the very concept of "an object." The construction begins when the infant starts to coordinate various action schemes—for example, hearing and looking at the same object; reaching and grasping the same object; seeing, reaching, and grasping the same object; reaching, grasping, and sucking the same object. In order to construct the object scheme from those experiences, he must abstract from them the one feature that they all share—the one *invariant* among many experiences—namely, the special configuration of experiences that is characteristic of that particular object. In the initial stages of that construction, each object with which the child interacts is to him merely a temporary node in a network of sensorimotor activities.

Progress toward acquisition of *the concept of the permanent object* can be detected by observing the child's behavior in a certain kind of situation: an object to which he has been visually attending is suddenly removed from his visual field. A very young infant in that situation promptly shifts his attention to something else; he does not search for the object at all, because when he ceases to *act* on it (in this case, look at it) as far as he is concerned it ceases to exist. Later, he does search briefly, but very briefly and only in one modality. (If he has been looking at the object, he looks for it when it disappears; if he has been handling it, he gropes for it manually; and so on.) After the various sensory modalities have been coordinated, the infant will engage in cross-modal searching; but a very strange thing happens if you hide an object in one place several times and then, without concealment of any kind, move it from there to another place a foot or two from the first.[1] He looks for it at the place where it *first* disappeared! There is a kind of "overpermanence" here, as though the central process representing the object is firmly tied to others representing its immediate surroundings. To put it another way, the infant sees "the object-I-find-at-A" being hidden, and he fails to assimilate the object to its new hiding place.[2] He has not yet constructed a stable *object concept* out of his experiences with objects in many settings.

Later, the child is able to follow displacements of an object if they are visible; but, if you conceal it as you move it from one place to another, he will again look for it where it first disappeared. Finally, toward the end of the period, the child searches for the object in the *last* place first, then in the other places where you might have hidden it. The object concept now remains stable in the face of momentary changes in the sensory field (seeing an object from various angles and distances, seeing it disappear behind a screen, and so on); it is an equilibrated system.

Closely related to the permanence of objects is the construction of space and time dimensions. Space, especially, is a relationship among objects, and objects exist in space. When there are no objects, there is no space, and vice versa. Both depend on the coordination of actions such as looking and seeing, and reaching and grasping and further coordinations such as looking-seeing-reaching-grasping-sucking. As the infant becomes more adept at those coordinations, he begins to move objects about, and eventually his interest expands to include relations among objects, as opposed to an exclusive concern with his actions on each object individually.

That expansion is the beginning (barely the beginning) of a conception of *general space.*

One result is that by about the end of his first year, the child has acquired the ability to reverse an object in space. For example, earlier, when handed a bottle backward, the infant would make no effort to turn it around; now, he immediately reverses it so that the nipple is toward him. It will be a long time before he can imagine what an object looks like from someone else's point of view, but this does seem to be a step in that direction.

In the last part of the Sensorimotor (it might be better classified as the first of the Preoperational) Period, the child begins to construct *symbols* to represent his environment internally. Now he can think about *absent* objects or about present ones in other settings. For example, if he rolls a ball under a sofa, he is able to turn away from the now-invisible ball's trajectory in order to circumnavigate the barrier and pick up the ball on the other side. That performance requires not only internal representation of the ball in its new environment, but also a remarkably effective coordination of action schemes (for example, if the ball moves north, then walking east, north, and west will complete a cycle of displacements that began with the moving of the ball). That coordination constitutes a further refinement of the child's concept of space.

So permanent objects and space are two aspects of the same construction. But there is at least one more such aspect: *time.* The very idea of "permanence" implies a temporal dimension; so as object permanence (and with it space) develops, so does the conception of time. The behavioral manifestations of the one also imply the other. At first an object exists only briefly, if at all, and when it disappears there is only a brief search for it; later, the search is more prolonged. At first, the child loses track of an object as soon as it is hidden; later, he can follow a sequence of displacements. At first, he lives only in the present; later, he both remembers past events and anticipates future ones. He has achieved a rudimentary conception of time.

Intention, Means—End Relations, and Causality

Before he will say that an act is *intentional,* Piaget requires that it show three characteristics:

1. Object-centered orientation
2. Intermediate act *(means)* preceding goal act *(end)*
3. Deliberate adaptation to new situations

The behavior of very young infants often manifests an object-centered orientation (although as we noted earlier, it is always brief). But the separation of means from ends and the deliberate adaptation to new situations do not occur so promptly. The first clear evidence of them does not appear until near the end of the first year: If you present a ten-month-old with an attractive trinket and then interpose a barrier between him and it, he will probably set about deliberately (1) to remove the barrier and (2) to reach for the trinket.[3] When he was younger, he would have lost interest in the object as soon as it disappeared behind the barrier. (Why shouldn't he; it didn't *exist* for him then!) Now, he "deliberately adapts to a new situation" by separating means from end and executing the two acts in sequence.

It is also at about this time that we see the first clear indications of a construction that is anything like what an adult means by *causality.* Previously, the infant was involved initially in every transaction that made any impression on him; now, he can perceive objects other than himself as causes. The evidence for this is that he sometimes attacks barriers (as if they were "causing" his frustration). There is an expansion of interest from the action alone to the action and its effect. On the stimulus side, he sometimes waits for adults to do things for him (again in recognition of a "cause" outside himself).

In the latter half of the Sensorimotor Period, the child engages in what many psychologists call "trial-and-error" behavior. Piaget calls it "groping accommodation." The following example will suffice to show why.

Piaget's daughter Jacqueline is imprisoned in a play pen. The vertical bars of the pen are 6 centimeters apart, and there is a stick 20 centimeters long lying outside, perpendicular to the bars. In her first attempt to bring it in, Jacqueline grasps the stick firmly in the middle and pulls. Of course, the stick stays outside, because the bars prevent its entry. In the ensuing several trials, she (1) tries to pull it through horizontally by grasping it in the middle, as in the first trial, (2) pulls it through horizontally by grasping one of its ends, and (3) pulls it through by rotating it to the vertical position. Eventually, she settles on this last technique and tilts it consistently *before* pulling.[4]

Apparently Jacqueline's initial response is an assimilation of the new situation to an already well established reaching-grasping-pulling scheme. And what she is eventually able to achieve, after a considerable amount of groping, is an accommodation of that scheme to the presence of the vertical bars. She *elaborates new means* (changes in the grasping point and the pulling angle) to achieve the end of acquiring an object. Later on, the child invents still other means to that end. For example, she learns to use one object to acquire another object, as when she draws a toy toward her with a stick.[5]

The elaboration of means also has a causative significance. When the child uses a stick or a string to pull something toward him, he is constrained to discriminate between himself and the tool as the immediate cause of the object's movement. This represents another step away from his original "the-world-is-my-actions-on-it" conception of reality.

That trend continues as the child develops the ability to represent external events internally. As we have seen, that ability is part and parcel of the integration of time and space. It, too, has significance for causality, for it makes possible the imagining of the cause of an effect (as when an object appears out of nowhere dangling from one end of a long stick and the child *knows* there is someone standing behind him holding the other end of the stick)[6] and of the effect of a cause (as when he knows that an adult will remove him from his play pen if he indicates that he needs to use the toilet).[7] Before the end of his second year, our subject apparently is capable not only of inferring a cause from its effect but also of foreseeing the effect of a cause. Notice that both of those depend on the extension of time and space coordinates described earlier. That extension is accompanied by and is necessary to, a more sophisticated conception of causality.

Imitation

You may recall that Piaget conceives of intellectual development as changes in structure through the actions of assimilation and accommodation. It happens that *im-*

itation is nearly pure accommodation and play is almost entirely assimilation. That makes imitation and play especially interesting to anyone who is studying those "invariant functions," as they are called. Imitation is especially important because aside from perception it is *the* foundation of the figurative aspect of thinking. (Images are even more important, but they are really internalized imitations.)

Before the appearance of imitation proper, there occurs a process called *pseudoimitation:* If someone does something the infant has just done, the infant imitates the imitation. That is not true imitation; it is merely assimilation, into an already established scheme, of the other's action as though it were his own.

The first true imitation looks rather like pseudoimitation because it consists entirely of actions that are already in the infant's repertoire. The difference is that the action does not have to be initiated by the infant. If he has waved "bye-bye" many times in the past but not recently, he may do so again now, if you do it first. He reproduces only familiar patterns, however, and his actions still include as much assimilation as accommodation. Moreover, the movements imitated must be visible on his own body.

So far, the child's own actions and those of the model are relatively undifferentiated, as you can see. But toward the end of the first year, you will recall, the child's general development includes the construction of the permanent object as an entity distinct from his own activity. After that, his view of the model's actions is quite different from what it had been previously. "Instead of appearing to be continuations of his own activity, they are now partially independent realities that are analogous to what he himself can do and yet distinct from it."[8] Once that change has occurred, the child develops an interest in novel actions and begins to imitate them.

In the last six months of the Sensorimotor Period (the part that is sometimes classified with the Preoperational Period), the child's behavior manifests three advances over his previous accommodations. He now imitates

1. Complex new models without extensive trial and error
2. Nonhuman, even nonliving, objects.
3. Absent objects

The imitation of nonhuman objects is important both because it serves the investigator as an indication that representation is going on, and because it can serve the child as the representation itself. When Jacqueline's doll gets caught by its feet in the top of her dress, she extricates it, with difficulty; but as soon as she gets it out, she tries to put it back again, apparently in an effort to understand what has happened. Failing in this, she crooks her forefinger into the shape of the doll's foot and places it under the neck of her dress. After pulling briefly with the imprisoned finger, she removes it, apparently satisfied. Piaget interprets this as the construction of "a kind of active representation of the thing that had just happened and that she did not understand."[9]

Imitation of absent objects—called *deferred imitation*—is important because it marks the beginning of "the semiotic function" that will be the main focus of our discussion in the next chapter. The illustration that I have in mind will be presented in the following section. The reason for presenting an example of imitation in a section on play will be made clear in that section.

Play

Imagine imitation and play near the two poles of a dimension that reaches from pure accommodation to pure assimilation. (The poles themselves are only abstractions; they do not correspond to anything that ever really happens.) We have followed the development of imitation—mostly accommodation. Now we shall do the same for play—predominantly assimilation.

Sometimes after an adaptive scheme has been constructed, it begins to function on its own, without regard to its original objective. Piaget cites the example of a child who has learned to throw his head back "to look at familiar things from this new position."[10] Having mastered that pattern, he begins to throw his head back without any apparent attention to what he can see by so doing. When the accommodation becomes subordinated to the assimilation, and the original "end" of the action drops out, the activity can be classified as play, because the "means" has become an end in itself.

A later example comes from Piaget's daughter Lucienne, who discovers that the objects hanging above her bed can be made to swing. At three and one-half months, she studies this phenomenon seriously, "with an appearance of intense interest." At four months, however, "she never indulges in this activity . . . without a show of great joy and power."[11] The serious work of comprehension, the main accommodative aspect of the act, has dropped out entirely. Except for perception, what is left is pure assimilation; it is play.

At the age of about one year, Piaget's other daughter, Jacqueline, notices the splash made by her hand as it slips accidentally from her hair while she is bathing. She immediately makes the touch-hair-hit-water-splash sequence into a game, which she then plays many times with great glee. Piaget calls this kind of game a "ritualization" of the scheme that organizes the action.[12] Some rituals are formed by dropping the accommodative component from an adaptive act; but others, like this one, never do have an accommodative component (excepting perception, of course).

The last half year of the Sensorimotor Period is, you recall, a transitional stage in which the child is able to represent to himself objects that are not present. That characteristic shows up in imitation and also in play; indeed, this kind of play *includes* imitation—*deferred* imitation, as in the following incident.

Lucienne accidentally falls backward on her cot. Seeing a pillow, she seizes it and presses it against her face as though sleeping on it. She smiles broadly and then, after a moment, sits up delightedly. That ends the game, but it is repeated many times during the day, even in places other than the cot and with no pillow available. Each time, she smiles, throws herself back, and presses her hands against her face as though the pillow were there.[13] From this behavior, any thoughtful observer will infer that the child is using *symbols*. That is what makes this stage transitional to the Preoperational Period. It should also be clear that this activity is an example not only of imitation, but of play as well.

Imitation in the Service of Play

It is in this transitional phase that imitation and play become fused, with the latter dominating the former but dependent on it for figurative content. The progress of representational functioning in general is manifested by the deferred imitation that is illustrated by our last example of play. Imitation of an absent object is an integral component of much of the play that we observe in the Preoperational Period. When a child is "playing house," for example, he imitates parental behavior that he has observed in the past. When he is playing "cowboy," he imitates models he has seen and heard on television or perhaps in a theater. In these examples, the imitations have already been mastered and are subsequently assimilated into the schemes of play. My own term for that relationship is "imitation in the service of play."

Meaning

The meaning of any given state of reality is determined by the schemes to which it is assimilated. Because early structures are simple and crude, so are early meanings. Because later structures are complex and refined, so are later meanings. Notable advances within the Sensorimotor Period include, in the order of their appearance,

1. Motor meaning*
2. Signal meaning*
3. Symbol meaning.*

Motor Meaning

At around the middle of the first year, when the infant sees an object on which he has habitually performed some particular act in the past, he recognizes the object

---

*These terms are mine, not Piaget's.

by performing the act again, but often at a distance and always in abbreviated form. Lucienne sees two plastic parrots that have previously hung from the hood of her bassinet, where they would move whenever she did. Now when she sees them hung from a chandelier, she shakes her legs in recognition. Piaget interprets the shaking as recognition because of the distance separating Lucienne from the parrots and because of the brevity of the action. ("It is an outline of some action suggested by the sight.") So the action is not a misguided attempt to move the parrots; rather, "it is only a sort of acknowledgment."[14] The structures that represent the parrots are action schemes. There undoubtedly are others (such as "looking"); this shaking scheme is merely the most conspicuous. But these actions all have one thing in common: they are all detectable if you observe carefully, for they are all overt. They constitute a kind of *motor meaning*.

Signal Meaning

Signal meaning, however, has a component that is internal. By the age of about ten months, Jacqueline has learned to open her mouth for a spoon that comes from a glass of grape juice (which she likes very much) and to clamp it shut when the spoon comes from a bowl of soup (which she dislikes). Her mother tries to deceive her by taking a spoonful of soup and "passing it by the glass" on the way to an open mouth. But Jacqueline is not fooled; "she notes by the sound whether the spoonful comes from the glass or the bowl and obstinately closes her mouth [when it comes from the bowl]."[15] In another example of the same phenomenon, Jacqueline cries whenever her mother puts on a hat, because putting on a hat is part of a going-away ritual.

Earlier, the infant had acknowledged the presence of an object by reactivating some bit of overt behavior that had previously occurred in its presence; that bit of behavior was the "meaning" of the object. Now, the meaning is partly internal, and the reaction is not to sensory patterns as such (the glass, the bowl, and the hat) but to components of the total situation that are not being sensed at the moment (grape juice, soup, mother's departure). One stimulus event has become a *signal* for the total situation. I say "event" instead of "object" because an object is just one kind of event, and signification can involve other kinds. As Pavlov taught his dogs to salivate to a sound, that sound (which was not itself an object) became a signal for food. Similarly, in the present examples the sound of the glass or of the bowl is but one aspect of an object. It is nevertheless capable, by this stage of the child's development, of activating schemes that represent not only the object but the even more inclusive "situation" of which *it* is a part.

Symbol Meaning

The last six months or so of the Sensorimotor Period mark a transition of prime importance to intellectual development. If you will reread the concluding paragraphs of each of the preceding major sections ("Object Permanence, Space, and Time"; "Intention, Means–End Relations, and Causality"; "Imitation"; and "Play" of this chapter, you will find in each a reference to an ability that had been only hinted at before the last stage of the period: the ability to represent internally certain events that are not currently impinging on the child's sense organs. It is this new ability that gives this new kind of meaning its name. A *symbol* is something that suggests or represents something else.

It is also this new ability that has blurred the distinction between the Sensorimotor and Preoperational Periods as they are presented in Table 1.1. Even Piaget has suggested that the last several months of the former might better be included in the latter because of the contribution of those months to the development of "the semiotic function," because that development is the major achievement of the Preoperational Period.

Summary

Even if you were interested exclusively in the later periods of development, the Sensorimotor Period would be an excellent place to begin your study of intellectual development. The subject matter is more tangible here than it will be later. In particular, you can follow the interplay of assimilation and accommodation—the operative and figurative aspects of knowing—from the reflexive assimilation of isolated bits of physical reality, through the construction of permanent objects in space and time, to the beginnings of symbolic thinking. What you have learned here will serve you well as you examine what is built on this foundation.

Notes

1. Piaget, *The Construction of Reality in the Child* (1937 [1954]), p. 53.

2. Gratch, Appel, Evans, LeCompte, and Wright, "Piaget's Stage IV Object Concept Error" (1974), p. 72.

3. Piaget, *The Origins of Intelligence in Children* (1936 [1952]), pp. 216–219.

4. *Ibid.*, pp. 305–306.

5. *Ibid.*, pp. 33–36.

6. Piaget, *The Construction of Reality in the Child* (1937 [1954]), pp. 295–296.

7. *Ibid.*, p. 297.

8. Piaget, *Play, Dreams, and Imitation in Childhood* (1945 [1951]), p. 50.

9. *Ibid.*, p. 65.

10. *Ibid.*, p. 91.

11. *Ibid.*, p. 92.

12. *Ibid.*, p. 93.

13. *Ibid.*, pp. 96–97.

14. Piaget, *The Origins of Intelligence in Children* (1937 [1954]), pp. 186–187.

15. *Ibid.*, p. 249.

3

The Preoperational Period (2–7 Years)

3

The Preoperational Period (2–7 Years)

Intelligence might well be defined as the organization of adaptive behavior, and adaptive behavior is definitely different in the new period. The Sensorimotor child is action-oriented; he is limited to the pursuit of concrete goals. The Preoperational child can reflect on his own behavior—that is, on the organization of his behavior as it relates to the goal rather than merely on the goal itself (although, as we shall presently see, he does very little reflecting, and he cannot conceive of any other such reflection being different from his own).

Whereas the Sensorimotor child is limited to linking successive perceptions of concrete objects and events through very *brief* anticipations of the future and memories of the past, the Preoperational child has access to a comprehensive representation of reality that can include past, present, and future and can occur in an exceedingly short period of time. Piaget likens Sensorimotor intelligence to a motion picture both taken and projected very slowly so that "all the pictures are seen in succession, and so without the continuous vision necessary for understanding the whole."[1] The Preoperational child has achieved partial freedom from that limitation (although he is still restricted to representations of states, as distinguished from transformations, and his thinking generally lacks flexibility in comparison to later periods). And what is true of time is also true of space. The Sensorimotor child lives not only in the *now* but in the *here and* now, and breaking out of that confinement constitutes a developmental task of monumental importance.

Advances

An essential component of this extension in scope and of the shift of interest from action to explanation is the development of the signs and symbols that make it all possible.

The Semiotic* Function

The essential difference between a child in the Sensorimotor Period and one in the Preoperational Period is that the former is relatively restricted to *direct interactions* with the environment, whereas the latter is capable of manipulating *symbols* that *represent* the environment. As was brought out earlier, however, the foundations of

---

*Pertaining to signs and symbols.

symbolic activity are laid during the Sensorimotor Period.* It was shown that "motor meaning" develops in Stage 3, a quasi-symbolic meaning in Stage 4, and that in Stage 6 even the beginnings of symbol manipulation can be detected. Indeed, Piaget has even referred at least once to "the period of sensori-motor intelligence" as lasting "until about 18 months,"[2] which is six months earlier than the norm cited in Table 1.2.

The Preoperational child has *signifiers* (such as words and images) in his repertoire, and can differentiate them from *significates* (internalized "representations in the broadest sense" of earlier experiences to which the words or images may refer), whereas the Sensorimotor child apparently perceives the signal and the rest of the situation as a single unit—for example, "tinkle-on-bowl-taste-of-soup," or "hat-on-mother-go-away," or even "pillow-thumb-sleep." Piaget sometimes refers to such a signal as an *index*. An index is an undifferentiated part of a total situation, as for example the visible part of an object that is otherwise hidden behind a screen. Once Pavlov had conditioned his dogs to salivate to a sound, that sound had become an index. In each case, the sub-

---

*Piaget is not consistent in his use of the term *symbol*. In a single paragraph,[3] he says of the "ritualizations" of Stages 4 and 5 that "such actions are certainly not yet properly called symbolic, since the action is only a reproduction of itself and is therefore both signifier and signified," and then refers to those same rituals as "symbols" that serve as a preparation for the "representational symbols" that emerge later on. Perhaps the best recourse here is to place emphasis not on the change toward symbolic representations, but on the increasing differentiations of signifier from significate (that which is signified); though again the issue is clouded, for Piaget sometimes includes the latter in his definition of the former.[4]

ject responds to the index as if it *were* the total situation. The "signal meaning" of the Sensorimotor Period is of that kind.

The Preoperational child, on the other hand, can make an internal response that represents an absent object or event. And he can differentiate that signifier (an internal process that represents tinkle-on-bowl, hat-on-mother, or pillow and thumb-sucking) from its significate (the process that represents taste-of-soup, mother-go-away, or going to sleep).

To summarize, then: entrance into the Preoperational Period is marked by increasing internalization of representational actions and increasing differentiation of signifiers from significates. Development of the semiotic function is an enormous step in the direction of cognitive autonomy—the independence of thinking from its Sensorimotor origins.

Origins of the Semiotic Function

But thinking does have Sensorimotor origins, and tracing them serves as a review of the processes of accommodation, which produces the *figurative* aspect of knowledge, and assimilation, which produces the *operative* aspect.

Accommodation

The semiotic function has a great future; but what about its past? How did it get started? Probably the most important notion here is that of "internalized imitation." Just as absent events were "re-presented" in the Sensorimotor Period by overt imitations triggered by sensory input (deferred imitation), so the representation is now accomplished covertly by means of an imitation that has been made in the past and internalized. This, then, is the "signifier": it signifies the event that was imitated and thus provides the *figurative* aspect of the child's knowledge of the event.

Assimilation

All of what has just been said refers, of course, to accommodation. How does assimilation fit in? Simply by being what it is: the process of signifying *is* essentially an assimilatory process—it is the process of supplying the significate when the signifier is evoked. Or, to put it another way, the signifier acquires meaning when it is assimilated to the schemes that represent the signified event—to the corresponding significate. That is the *operative* aspect of knowing.

As an example, do you remember when Jacqueline's doll got caught by its feet on the edge of her blouse? After extricating it, she used her finger to represent the doll's foot as she hooked it into the same place, apparently studying the phenomenon that she had just discovered. She would know what to do, should it happen again. Another example is Lucienne's behavior when confronted with a problem that could be solved by opening a matchbox. The "opening plan" was represented by opening her mouth![5]

Those examples illustrate transitional problem-solving abilities. Later in the Preoperational Period, the motor loops drop out, and the whole process runs itself off without any perceptible movement.

Coordination of Assimilation and Accommodation

Actually, I have oversimplified this. Piaget classifies functions on the "representative" dimension as follows:

Accommodation
Effects of the present: simple accommodations
Effects of the past: representations and images

Assimilation
Effects of the present: incorporation of data into adequate schemes
Effects of the past: connections established between the present schemes and others whose meanings are merely evoked [recalled] and not provoked by present perception.[6]

My interpretation of that last effect is that the "present schemes" are the signifiers and the "others whose meanings are merely evoked" are the "significates" mentioned earlier.

The added time dimension is a complication that causes difficulty in the equilibration of assimilation and accommodation; and that, in turn, contributes to the well-known instability of the period, in which the child is continually shifting among play, imitation, and intelligent adaptation.*

But even in deliberately contrived problem-solving situations like the Piagetian "experiments" (such as the ones that we shall be examining shortly), the child's ad-

---

*One way of conceptualizing at least part of this instability is to think of the child as continually playing games, and that "reality is a game at which he is willing to play with adults and anyone else who believes in it."[7]

aptation is faulty by adult standards because his cognitive functioning is so unsystematic. There seems to be no metastructure to integrate substructures. So assimilation of one of the experimenter's displays to one scheme has no necessary implications for any other scheme and hence for the cognition that results from the next display. The outcome in each case is a flagrant logical contradiction—a contradiction that will be corrected when the schemes accommodate to each other as well as to the external environment, thus forming the "metastructure" mentioned earlier.

Summary of the Semiotic Function

From the amount of space that we have devoted to the semiotic function in this chapter, you may well be wondering why we don't call this the "Semiotic Period" in honor of its major achievement. Actually, that might not be a bad idea if "Preoperational" had not achieved general acceptance as a name for the period. General acceptance is a virtue in itself, as you will no doubt agree after reading the following discussion.

Figure 3.1, like Figure 1.1 and Table 1.2, is an attempt to bring together a large number of concepts in order to indicate relationships among them. Throughout this summary, you will find it useful to follow the discussion on the chart; I have italicized key words to assist you in that.

Because operative intelligence encompasses a nearly infinite variety of *significates,* I have not attempted to classify them except by level. The Sensorimotor Period is missing because it lacks the signifier–significate relation that defines the semiotic function. The Preopera-

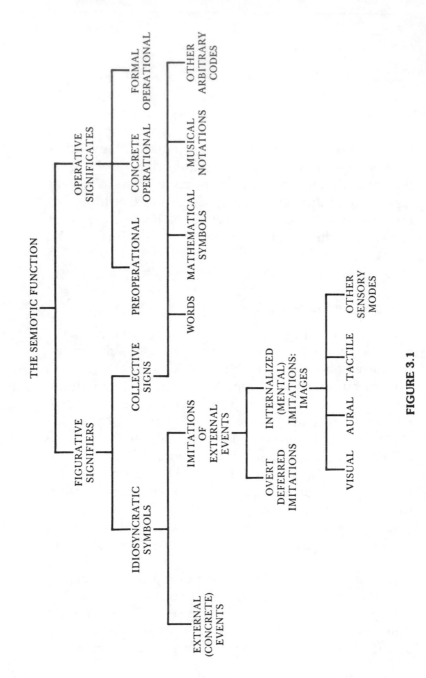

FIGURE 3.1

tional Period is, of course, the one we have been discussing in this chapter, and we shall be examining the two "operational" levels presently. Notice also that, although this operative intelligence is necessary to the functioning of *signifiers,* it is considered separate from them for purposes of analysis (in the same way that assimilation and accommodation are often treated separately, even though neither can occur without the other).

On the chart, signifiers are divided into two broad classes that Piaget calls respectively *symbols* and *signs.* The two differ with respect to their relations to significates:

1. "Symbol," in which the signifier is
   a. Usually similar to the significate
   b. Private, idiosyncratic
2. "Sign," in which the relation to the significate is
   a. Arbitrarily selected
   b. Socially ("collectively") agreed on

This is Piaget's own terminology. It differs from that of most other scholars (notably, linguists and psycholinguists), so in your other reading you may find that the same terms have different referents—even when, as sometimes occurs, those referents constitute essentially the same set of concepts as Piaget's.[8]

But let us accept Piaget's terminology and see what it can do for us. Symbols can be external (concrete) events, or they can be *imitations* of such events. If they are external events, they are usually *objects* that either bear some physical similarity to the significate (as a toy car does to a real one) or form some part of it (a pillow might signify bed—indeed, the whole bedtime routine, with all its cognitive and emotional components). The same is true if the symbols are overt imitations of external events (pressing a pillow against the face as if sleeping on it or pressing the hands against the face even in the absence of the pillow might signify that same bedtime routine); again, there is some intrinsic relation between the signifier and its significate. These are *deferred imitations;* they are only a step away from the internalized imitations that Piaget calls *images.* Because they are entirely internal, images have a degree of independence from environmental supports, with a resulting flexibility, that qualifies them for the designation *mental.*

In all of this, there has been at least some similarity between the signifier and the significate. (Some seashells *look* something like boats. Pressing hands against face in the absence of bed is figurally the same as in its presence, whether the action is overt or internal.) Also, although that similarity does influence a child's choice of a particular signifier, some other child may choose one that is similar to the same significate in a rather different way (a floating block of wood, for example). *Signs* are signifiers, too, but they are not similar to their significates, and they are not "idiosyncratic." The word *horse* does not look at all like a horse. Indeed, any other word would serve as well to signify that noble beast, providing only that we all agree just which word it is to be. Once agreement has been achieved, that word—that "sign"— can be used for communication among us. The word shares with the idiosyncratic "symbol" the function of representing absent objects, but it has in addition the capability of being communicated more or less explicitly from any one of us to any other one. Thus, with the advent of language, thinking becomes socialized.

Signifiers, Significates, and Language

Anyone who has ever thought about development has noticed the correlation of verbal ability with the general mental ability called "intelligence." But, since correlations are not causes, we are left with the question of what causes what.

Nevertheless, many people have asserted, on the basis of that relation, that "representational thought" results from the learning of words. Piaget does not agree with that view, for he points out that the first signifiers are not linguistic signs, but rather private symbols for which there are no signs. The shaking of Lucienne's legs represents the bassinet fringe; lying down and pressing her hands against her face represents going to sleep; opening and closing her mouth represents opening and closing a match box; the hooking of Jacqueline's finger around the edge of her blouse represents a doll's foot caught in the same place.

Those are all *imitations*. When the imitations become internalized, Piaget calls them "images," and those images are the first internal signifiers. The significates are their meanings for a particular child; they are the operative aspects of knowing.

Identify, if you can, the signifiers and the significates in the following short observation.

Observation 77
At twenty-one months Jacqueline saw a shell and said "cup." After saying this, she picked it up and pretended to drink. (She had often pretended to drink with various objects, but in these instances the object was assimilated to the drinking schema. Here the identification of the shell with the cup preceded the action.) The next day,

seeing the same shell, she said "glass," then "cup," then "hat," and finally "boat in the water." Three days later she took an empty box and moved it to and fro saying "motycar."[9]

The signifiers are the child's internalized imitations of a shell or of a box. The significates are the models of earlier experiences—the "schemes"—to which the image of the shell or of the box can be assimilated. Another possibility would be for the image of a shell to be assimilated to the concept of a shell—to a scheme that represents the common features of many "shell experiences" of the past. But in the episode Piaget describes here, the signifier process "shell" is assimilated by the scheme of "cup" in one instance, of "hat" in another, and of "boat" in still another—with some accommodation of each scheme to the image, of course.

To put it another way, the meanings of the shell consist of the schemes to which it can be assimilated. Words are imitations, too; they serve as signifiers, and their meanings are similarly determined. The words used by Jacqueline in this example refer not to the conventional meaning of "shell," but to the idiosyncratic meanings that reside in this particular subject. Often the referent of a noun is not an object at all, but an action or class of actions. "Mommy" may refer to a large class of helping behaviors, and in certain contexts it means, "Help me!" Or the child may invent words to fit developed concepts. Examples are "It's raining and winding out," "Let me key the door," or "I can do it 'cause he teached me."

Apparently what the Preoperational child does is to assimilate words into his already established idiosyncratic system of significates. Later on, language will have an important role within the symbolic function; for a language provides a ready-made notation for many "operational" instruments (classification, conservation, and so on, and especially propositional logic) such as those we shall encounter in Chapters 4 and 5. But for now, words serve as signifiers for significates that do not yet form the coherent systems that will characterize them later.

Limitations

We have been looking at the Preoperational Period from a perspective gained by first studying the Sensorimotor Period. In short, we have compared this period with the one that preceded it. That is a defensible procedure, of course; but since we are all inclined to take our own intellectual processes for granted, it may be useful to point out ways in which the child's thought is still quite different from that of a normal adult.

I shall explore those limitations of Preoperational thought under six headings (even though Piaget himself has not done so, and there probably could be many more). The six are

1. Concreteness
2. Irreversibility
3. Egocentrism
4. Centering
5. States versus transformations
6. Transductive reasoning

Inasmuch as Piaget coined these terms during the course of many years of research and writing, it should not be surprising to find much redundancy in any list of this length. In fact, that is what we do find; in many ways, his categories represent different ways of referring to essentially the same thing.

It may be appropriate in the introduction to a section on the inadequacies of preoperational thinking to mention once again that hoary controversy concerning the role of language in thinking. Wordsworth expressed beautifully (as poets are wont to do) one point of view in that regard: "The word," he said, "is not the dress of thought, but its very incarnation."

Not so, says Piaget. Language is the vehicle by which thought is socialized, but it is not the original basis of, nor does it ever become the whole of, human thinking. Our analysis of intellectual development will therefore not be concerned exclusively or even primarily with the development of language. Conversely, the limitations that we shall examine are not primarily linguistic limitations.

Concreteness

You may well be wondering why the Preoperational child is here characterized as "concrete" when the ability to manipulate "symbols" is the main feature that differentiates this period from the one that preceded it. The answer is that compared to the behavior of the Sensorimotor infant, the behavior of the child who has reached the Preoperational Period *is* relatively independent of momentary sensory inputs. But compared to an adolescent or adult, he is still very concrete-minded indeed.

Much of his thinking takes the form of what Piaget calls *mental experiment.* Instead of the adult pattern of analyzing and synthesizing, the Preoperational child simply runs through the symbols for events as though he were actually participating in the events themselves. As compared to more advanced levels, his thinking at this stage tends to be dominated by its figural aspects— by perceptions and images.

In special circumstances, even adult thinking may be dominated by its figurative aspect. You can demonstrate that to yourself by taking the following brief psycho-motor test:

> Place the butt end of a pencil or a pen within the alley at the very top of Figure 3.2. Your object is to reach the center of the spiral as quickly as possible without leaving that alley. Now look at your watch, note carefully what the time will be at the next even minute, and then, at exactly the time you have noted, begin.

FIGURE 3.2

How long did it take? Did you finish? If not, then you are now in a position to *think* of this figure as a series of concentric circles instead of a spiral. Having taken the prescribed "test," your thinking is no longer dominated by your perception; but you still can *perceive* it in only one way.

This is happening to you in this special condition,* but it happens all the time to a Preoperational child. He is unable, for example, to process information from the two bodies of liquid in Figure 1.2 as "same quantity," just as you were initially unable to process information from Figure 3.2 as "concentric circles." In both child and adult, *perception* is the dominant mental activity. (The figurative aspect dominates the operative aspect of knowing.) The difference between them is that when you discovered that the path did not lead to the center, *you could* conceptualize the figure in a new way; your mental processes exhibited mobility within a conceptual structure. The Preoperational child cannot do that; his thinking lacks that mobility, because it lacks that structure.

Irreversibility

"Reversible" means "capable of being returned to its point of origin"; every mathematical or logical operation is reversible. For example:

$3 + 5 = 8$, and
$8 - 5 = 3$.

---

*Piaget probably would say that "this special condition" is one in which "field effects" are especially strong. In this book, we shall not discuss his ideas about perception. Suffice it to say that, in *most* situations, perception gradually attains relative independence from such effects. Even perception evolves.

Or

all men and all women = all adults, and
all adults except women = all men.

You can

add something to the "3" and then
take it away.

You can

increase the size of the group and then
decrease it again.

In each case, you have

thought your way from one condition to another and
returned to the starting point.

That is the defining characteristic of reversible thought. It is *not* a characteristic of the thought of a Preoperational child.

Note also that each of these changes is a part of a closed system in which any change in one part of the system requires a compensating change in some other part. For example:

If 3 + 5 = 8 and
I increase the "3" by one,
I must also decrease the "5" by the same amount if I am
to stay within the system—the system of two numbers
whose sum is "8."

It is of course not surprising that the Preoperational child cannot accomplish this reversal; after all, he hasn't been yet taught arithmetic. But here is a problem that does not demand such special skill (see Figure 3.3):

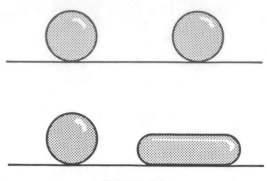

FIGURE 3.3

Two plasticene balls of equal size are shown to a child. He is asked,

"Are they the same size, or
does one have more plasticene in it than the other?"

He says they are the same. Then—right before his very eyes—one of the balls is rolled into a sausage shape and he is asked the same question as before. This time he says that one has more plasticene than the other! Usually he says the sausage is the larger, but sometimes it is the ball. In Piaget's terms, he fails to *conserve* "substance"*— he fails to continue to think of the amount of clay as the same while its length and width are changing.

Why should a transformation performed entirely within his visual field and with his full attention produce such a result? One reason is that the child's thinking cannot reverse itself back to the point of origin. He can "see" neither (1) that, because nothing has been either added or removed, the sausage could be made back into the original ball, nor (2) that every change in height is compensated by a change in breadth, leaving the total quantity what it was in the beginning. Those failures constitute two kinds of irreversibility.

---

*"Substance" is sometimes called "mass," sometimes "matter," sometimes simply "quantity."

Another example very similar to the plasticene-ball problem consists of comparing two equal amounts of liquid or two equal numbers of wooden beads in containers of different shape. Let us assume that beads are used.*

The child is given a pile of beads; he is then asked to pick up one in each hand,

to put the one in the left hand into Container *A*,
to put the one in the right hand into Container *B*, and
to continue until there are no more pairs to pick up.

But Containers *A* and *B* are differently shaped, as shown in Figure 3.4. And when the subject is asked, "Which has the larger number of beads,

Container *A*, or
Container *B*, or
do they both contain the same amount?"

his answer is "There's more in this one," and he points sometimes to *A*, but usually to *B*. (Just which one it is depends on "centering,"[11] which will soon be discussed. Occasionally a subject will make his judgment on the basis not of one or the other dimension of the material itself but of the sizes of the containers: "This one has more because the jar is bigger." It is as though the child's internal representations of quantities of materials are assimilated into his representation of the containers that hold them. (See the discussion of "transductive reasoning" on pp. 90–95.)

---

*This makes it a test of conservation of discontinuous rather than of continuous quantity. I shall nevertheless refer henceforth to both of these problems (beads and liquid) together as "the water-level problem."[10] For a description of the liquid version, turn back to p. 30.

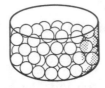

CONTAINER *A*   CONTAINER *B*

FIGURE 3.4

The young child makes what to us are startling errors in thinking even about simple transpositions that occur within his field of vision. He does so mainly because his thinking is *irreversible*.

Egocentrism

Just as the early Sensorimotor child was "egocentric" in his overt actions ("the world is my actions on it"), so the Preoperational child is egocentric in his representations ("the world is as it looks to me").

The term *egocentric* is used not in a pejorative sense, but descriptively, to refer to his inability to take another person's point of view. He will speak to you using words that have idiosyncratic referents and using associations unrelated to any discernible logical structure; and then he'll be very much surprised when he fails to communicate. He is surprised because he cannot understand how you can see it any way but his way.

The ability to take the view of the other (without losing

his own) and the corresponding social norm of logical consistency will be acquired partly as by-products of the child's construction of a well-articulated model of the physical world *via* myriad interactions with that world. It will be a model that is characterized by stable *relationships* among objects. But its development will also depend on repeated social interactions in which the child is compelled again and again to take account of the viewpoints of others. This social feedback is extremely important in developing the capacity to think objectively about his own thinking, a capacity without which logic is impossible.

Centering

One way to describe egocentrism is "centering on one's own view of the moment." Related to that and all other Preoperational characteristics is the one called *centering, or centration.*[12] It refers to the child's tendency to center his attention on one detail of an event and hence his inability to process information from other aspects of the situation. That inability is characteristic of the Preoperational child, and it has a disturbing effect on his thinking, as you may well imagine.

In the water-level problem, for example, he will center on either the height of the container (and say that the tall one is larger) or the width (and say that the wide one is larger). If it were possible for him to *de*center in this problem, he could take into account both the height and the width, and that would allow him to relate the changes in one of those dimensions to compensatory changes in the other.

But the Preoperational child cannot decenter, and— at least partly for that reason—cannot solve the problem.

States Versus Transformations

Also related to deployment of attention is the Preoperational child's tendency to center on the successive *states* of a display without noting the *transformations* by which one state is changed into another. Looking at the water-level problem with this tendency in mind, it is easy to see how it might hinder the child's thinking. The transformation by itself would give an adult a feeling of certainty that the water poured from one beaker to another is the same water. But it doesn't do that for the child. It is as though he were viewing a series of still pictures instead of the movie that the adult sees.

A dramatic illustration of this comes from an experiment in which the subject's task was "to depict (by actual drawings or by multiple-choice selection of drawings) the successive movements of a bar that falls from a vertical, upright position to a horizontal one."[13] A correct sequence would look something like that shown in Figure 3.5. That sequence is of course obvious to an adult, but the young child commonly fails to draw the intermediate positions of the stick—or sometimes even to recognize them when they are shown to him.

Preoperational children have much difficulty with this simple—and, to an adult, obvious—action sequence. They are unable to integrate a series of states or conditions into a coherent whole—namely, a *transformation*.

Transductive Reasoning

We noted the gradual development, during the Sensorimotor Period, of a conception of causality. Transitional between that and the reasoning of the adult is what Piaget calls "preconceptual" or "transductive" reasoning. Since Piaget is a logician as well as a psychologist, I prefer

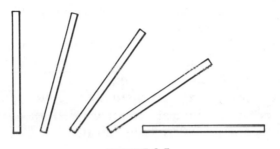

FIGURE 3.5

not to argue with him when he calls it "reasoning," but it certainly doesn't follow the familiar rules we know as reason. Instead of proceeding from the particular to the general (induction), or from the general to the particular (deduction),* the Preoperational child proceeds

---

*Probably the most often-used illustration of deductive reasoning is

All men are mortal.   (general)

Socrates is a man; therefore Socrates is mortal.   (particular)

An inductive complement might be

Our observations indicate that until now every
man we have observed (including Socrates) has
died before reaching the age of 150; that is, all
men have been mortal.   (particular)

It is reasonable to infer that all men are mortal.   (general)

This is a common way of distinguishing between deductive and inductive arguments; indeed, it seems to be implied by the words *de*ductive and *in*ductive. But it is not the only way. Robert Baum, for example, defines a deductively valid argument as one in which the premises imply the conclusion absolutely and an inductive argument as one that is not deductively valid.[14] Since a transductive argument is deductively invalid, Baum's *in*duction subsumes Piaget's *trans*duction.

from particular to particular (transductive reasoning) without any reference to the general.

The result is sometimes a correct conclusion, as it was when Jacqueline, at thirty months, twenty-seven days said, "Daddy's getting hot water, so he's going to shave."[15] (Here she merely repeats mentally a sequence that she has experienced physically; no new relation is constructed.) But sometimes it is rather strange:

Observation 111
At two years, fourteen days, Jacqueline wanted a doll-dress that was upstairs: she said "Dress," and her mother refused to get it, "Daddy get dress." As I also refused, she wanted to go herself "To mommy's room." After several repetitions of this she was told that it was too cold there. There was a long silence, and then: "Not too cold." [I asked] "Where?" "In the room." "Why isn't it too cold?" "Get dress."[16]

The reader may object that this is merely common childish insistence on getting what he wants. That may be true, but it is just that common childish behavior that Piaget is trying to explain—or at least to classify. The fact is that childish insistence is qualitatively different from adult insistence. Piaget characterizes the child's thinking in this example as "a continuation, in a slightly more complicated form, of the practical coordinations of the baby of twelve to sixteen months—e.g., rolling a watch chain into a ball to make it go into a box, etc."[17] The baby used a sensorimotor coordination as a means to an end; the young child uses mental coordinations. It is important to note here that I said "mental," not "verbal" coordinations. Jacqueline is not manipulating her speech in order to manipulate her parents. She actually *believes* what she says; the thoughts themselves have been recruited to the service of a goal.

In one of the preceding examples, the child's so-called reasoning led to a correct conclusion; in the other, it did not. But in either case, the same plan was followed, namely:

"*A* causes *B*" is not different from
"*B* causes *A*."
"Daddy's shave requires hot water" is not different from "Hot water requires Daddy's shave."
"A warm room makes possible the fetching of a dress" is not different from
"The fetching of the dress makes the room warm."

Another, somewhat different, pattern that is also called "transductive reasoning" concerns the child's lack of a hierarchy of categories. Adults can comprehend, for example, a hierarchy like the one depicted in Figure 3.6.*

But here is Jacqueline, dealing with a similar hierarchy:

Observation 112
At twenty-five months, thirteen days, Jacqueline wanted to see a little hunchbacked neighbor whom she used to meet on her walks. A few days earlier she had asked why he had a hump, and after I had explained she said: "Poor boy, he's ill, he has a hump." The day before, Jacqueline had also wanted to go and see him, but he had influenza, which Jacqueline called being "ill in bed." We started out for our walk and on the way Jacqueline

---

*Some Formal Operations adults fumble this one badly—for example, when they categorize as genetically inferior a minority group whose members have lacked learning opportunities. But Formal Operations adults are intellectually capable of doing better than that.

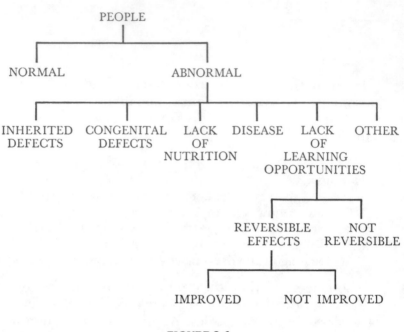

FIGURE 3.6

said: "Is he still ill in bed?" "No. I saw him this morning, he isn't in bed now." "He hasn't a big hump now!"[18]

Figure 3.7 shows the hierarchical pattern that must be built up in a person's mind before he can deal effectively with this type of problem. Jacqueline blithely transfers "recovery" in *A* to recovery in *B,* because her thinking lacks that hierarchical structure.

The reasoning is by simile:

A is like *B* in some way; therefore
A is like *B* in every way.*

---

*Again, this is a fairly accurate picture of the rigidity that can be found in the thinking of many adults in certain situations (for example, *A* and *B* both have dark skins; *B* is shiftless and irresponsible; therefore, so is *A*). Piaget has not dealt extensively with the question of why adult structures are not always used.

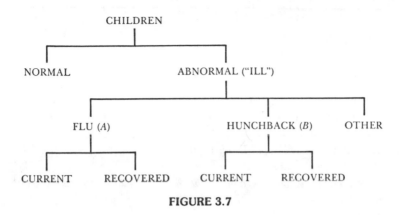

FIGURE 3.7

Or to put it another way (and this is roughly the way Piaget puts it)[19]; *A* is *assimilated* into *B*. The child is *centering* on *B*, and until he can decenter, his thinking will be characterized by a notable coarseness and rigidity— a lack of refinement and mobility—as compared to the operational thinking of the Concrete Operations Period.

Summary

The infant's world consists entirely of his own actions; objects exist only as aliments to his motor schemes. The Preoperational child lives in a more stable world, in that it is populated by the permanent objects that he constructed during his Sensorimotor Period, and he can deal mentally with objects and events that are distant in both time and space.

But the *relations* that he establishes among those objects and events are *not* so stable. They form only the beginnings of an equilibrated system for processing information about concrete reality. That system is brought to near perfection during the next period of development: the one called "Concrete Operations."

Notes

1. The official translation likens Sensorimotor intelligence to "a slow-motion film," but in a context that I believe clearly justifies my version. Piaget, *The Psychology of Intelligence* (1947 [1950]), p. 121.

2. Piaget, *The Child and Reality: Problems of Genetic Psychology* (1972 [1973]), p. 12.

3. Piaget, *Play, Dreams and Imitation in Childhood* (1945 [1951]), p. 101.

4. *Ibid.*, pp. 101–102.

5. *Ibid.*, p. 65.

6. *Ibid.*, p. 241.

7. *Ibid.*, p. 93.

8. For an illuminating discussion of this situation, see Furth's chapter on symbolic behavior in Furth, *Piaget and Knowledge* (1969).

9. Piaget, *Play, Dreams and Imitation in Childhood* (1945 [1951]), p. 124.

10. Piaget, *The Child's Conception of Number* (1941 [1952]), p. 25 ff.

11. Inhelder, "Criteria of the Stages of Mental Development" (1953), pp. 75–85.

12. *Ibid.*

13. Reported by Piaget in *Bulletin Psychologique, Paris* (1959), 12, 538–540, 574–576, 724–727, 806–807, 857–860. Cited by Flavell in his *The Developmental Psychology of Jean Piaget* (1963), p. 158. The words are Flavell's.

14. Baum, *Logic* (1975), pp. 19, 20.

15. Piaget, *Play, Dreams, and Imitation in Childhood* (1945 [1951], p. 231.

16. *Ibid.*

17. *Ibid.*, p. 233.

18. *Ibid.*, p. 231.

19. *Ibid.*, p. 235.

4

The Concrete Operations Period (7–11 Years)

4

The Concrete Operations Period (7–11 Years)

This is where schemes, which are "operative" by definition, become "operational." Piaget has defined an *operation* as "an action that can return to its starting point, and that can be integrated with other actions also possessing this feature of reversibility."[1] But an additional restriction should be included in the definition: the action is internalized. Flavell says that "any *representational* act that is an integral part of an organized network of related acts is an operation."[2] And finally, the resulting structures "give rise to a feeling of intrinsic necessity."[3] The reason for calling this new period "*concrete* operations" will become clear presently.

In Chapter 1, I suggested a "theme for the theory": the increasing independence of action from its immediate environment. Yet here we have an increasing systematizing of actions that results in "a feeling of necessity." In what sense can this be independence? As you read Chapters 4 and 5, find an answer to that question if you can.

Some Representative Problems

In discussing the Preoperational Period, I compared the cognitive processes of that period with those of the periods that precede and follow it. I shall be using a similar approach in this chapter to compare Preoperational functioning with Concrete Operational functioning in each of several different kinds of problems.

Classification

Conservation of serial, ordinal, and cardinal correspondence

Conservation of substance, weight, and volume

Egocentrism and decentering in the representation of objects

Egocentrism and decentering in social relations

Egocentrism and decentering in reasoning

Spatial relations

Distance, time, movement, and velocity

Actually, more time will be given in this section to Preoperational functioning than to Concrete Operational functioning, for there is no better way to develop an understanding and appreciation of the latter than to contrast it with the former. The various qualities of thought that have been discussed, and some that have not, will manifest themselves in the solutions to those problems.

Classification[4]

Even in the Sensorimotor Period, an infant may try out several schemes on a new object as if to "classify" it as an object to be squeezed, dropped, rubbed, and rattled (or all of these); but when the child achieves true classification, he is able to differentiate and to coordinate two crucial properties of a "class"; *intension* and *extension*.

"Intension" is the criterion—the quality that defines the class. "Extension" is the sum of all the objects that meet that criterion. The intension of the class "square cards" in Figure 4.1 would be "squareness," and its extension would be "four." Other possible classes from the display in Figure 4.1 are

intension "roundness," extension "five";
intension "black," extension "seven"; and
intension "white," extension "two."

In any fully equilibrated classification system, intension and extension must be completely coordinated. The intension of a class determines what objects may be included within it, and the objects that *are* in any collection

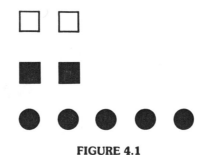

FIGURE 4.1

impose severe limits on additional attributes that *might* be used as criteria for classification. (If a set of squares includes white ones, for example, blackness cannot be required.)

Preoperational

The early Preoperational child is not yet capable of such coordination. He has had much experience with objects of many different kinds, and he has become aware of many attributes of those objects; but he is easily distracted by the *configuration* of an array, and even while he is actually working from a "similarities" base, he often includes objects that do not meet the class criterion, and he frequently changes the criterion.

When he is presented with a display like the one in Figure 4.2 and is asked to "put together those that are alike," the child may begin by placing objects together that are alike in one way, then continue doing the same

FIGURE 4.2

thing, but using a different attribute. He might begin sorting by shape and suddenly switch to color. Then, when he is halfway through, he may notice that his arrangement looks like a tree. After that, he will add objects in such a manner as to make it look more like a tree, completely ignoring both shape and color. (The result is called a *figural collection*.) Or he may group the objects on what appears to be a completely random basis (possibly because the child's criteria change so rapidly that no sorting at all is discernable to the adult observer). And finally, he may simply *omit* some objects from *all* of his collections.

Sometimes he *seems* to be using a classification strategy even when his mental functioning actually falls far short of that achievement. Wouldn't you be tempted to interpret the arrangement in Figure 4.3 in that way if your subject had constructed it by himself? That is, wouldn't you call it a product of "classification"? You would until you heard him say, "Choo choo"[!]

In that instance, his vocalizing gave him away, but even a child this young often will speak as though he comprehends important extensional concepts like "some" and "all." He may use the words with no hesitation; but, as will be shown, careful testing reveals that he lacks the clearly defined ideas to which they refer when an adult uses them.

For the early Preoperational child, a given intension does not determine any specific *extension*. He may begin putting *black* cards together but leave out some blacks

FIGURE 4.3

and finally throw in some *non*blacks; or he may appear to move the cards completely at random.

Later in the Preoperational Period he does much better. He seizes on a single attribute and sticks to it, and he applies it to *all* objects in the array. He may even set up what appears to be a *hierarchy* of categories of the type $A + A' = B$.

In Figure 4.2, A might be "white squares," and A' "black squares"; then B would be "squares," and B' would be "circles." Or A could be "circular blacks," and A' "square blacks"; then B would be "blacks," and B' would be "whites."

The child's arrangement might look just like Figure 4.1. Why, then, is Piaget reluctant to credit this child with true classification? The reason is that the subject's thinking still lacks the *inclusion relation,* which is Piaget's main criterion of true classification. Given the array of cards depicted in Figure 4.1, here is a simple test[5] that will prove it:

> E: "I'll take away the two white square cards and put them over here. (E removes two cards from the display depicted in Figure 4.1.) Now, if I were to take away all the *round* ones, would there be any cards left?"
>
> S: "Yes, the squares."
>
> E: "If I should take away all the *black* ones, would there be any cards left?"
>
> S: "No."
>
> E: "Which would make the bigger pile of cards, the round ones or the black ones?"
>
> S: "The round ones." [!]

That surely is a surprising response, from an adult point of view. It is surprising because adult thinking depends on structures that the Preoperational child does not have. In this example, an adequate structure might be something like that depicted in Figure 4.4.

According to the principle of composition, the class of black cards is part of the system that includes the round ones and the square ones, but for the Preoperational child that is not so. His approach to the problem is characterized by *centering* (on the shape criterion), *irreversibility* (from the parts back to the whole whence they came), and *transductive reasoning* (a part-to-part relation that excludes the part-to-whole relation). In those circumstances, it is impossible for him truly to comprehend the concepts "some" and "all."

Concrete Operations

According to Piaget, the faultless performances of the late Preoperational child in his other interactions with this array are indicative not of a *classificatory operation,* but merely of a "momentary differentiation of the collection of B into subcollections A and A'."[6]

An "operation" is by definition *reversible,* and it is not until somewhat later that the child is capable

not only of the *union,* $A + A' = B$,
but also of its *inverse,* $A = B - A'$,
or to put it another way, $B - A' = A$,
which is where he started (that is, with A).

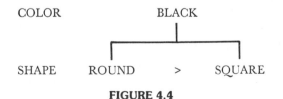

FIGURE 4.4

A Preoperational "collection" *(B)* ceases to exist when its subclasses are separated—either in space or only in thought, as they are when their extensions are compared. ("Are there more round ones or square ones?") The Concrete Operations "class" (also *B* in the equation) is stable and permanent; it will not disintegrate under any conditions.

Conservation of Serial, Ordinal, and Cardinal Correspondence: The Construction of Number

Parents often believe that when they teach their children to *count,* they are teaching them *numbers.* Actually, however, what the child is learning is primarily the figurative aspects of the number symbols. Often a pointing to one object after another is included in the "counting," and the pointing is coordinated with the verbalization; but then again, the child's knowledge is dominated by their figurative aspects. In other words, all a child learns when he learns to count is to make a series of sounds while pointing to the various members of a set of objects. For example, in the classification problem on pp. 102–106, the child might count the round cards or the black ones, or he might begin counting round ones and switch to black before he's through. He can "count," but he cannot "number" in the sense that Piaget uses the term.

Acquisition of a concept of number in that sense depends on the construction of a number system. The development of that system is spontaneous and predictable. Piaget has tested that development mostly by asking children to judge the numerical equivalence (one-to-one correspondence) of two sets of objects or to put one set into ordinal correspondence with another. When you are interpreting his results, however, it may help to note that the correspondence is important not so much for itself as for what it reveals about the child's conception of *one* of the sets in the display—namely, the set that is rearranged by the experimenter. Usually one of the sets is allowed to remain in its initial state while the other is either spread out or pushed together; if the subject reports that the number of items or the order of items in the rearranged set still corresponds to that of the unchanged set, we conclude that he regards the rearranged set to be, in those respects, also unchanged. He is said to have *conserved* those properties. In the face of irrelevant changes in the display, those properties remain unchanged. They are *invariants* in the display. Remember the construction of "the permanent object" in the Sensorimotor Period. There, the object itself was the invariant across many experiences; you could say that the object was "conserved." Here, some *attribute* of an object or set of objects (or of relations among those objects) is the invariant, and it is that attribute that is conserved.

This section is concerned with the conservation of one-to-one correspondence. There are at least three kinds of one-to-one correspondence: (1) *serial*, (2) *ordinal*, and (3) *cardinal*. The first two (serial and ordinal) can be illustrated in terms of a single experiment.

Experiment I: Dolls and Sticks
The child is presented with 10 dolls that differ in height and 10 sticks that also vary in length, but less so than the dolls do. He is told that the dolls are going for a walk and is asked to arrange the dolls and sticks "so that each doll can easily find the stick that belongs to it." If he succeeds in this, it will be by placing the two series parallel to each other, each in serial order of size, as indicated in Figure 4.5. But then the experimenter

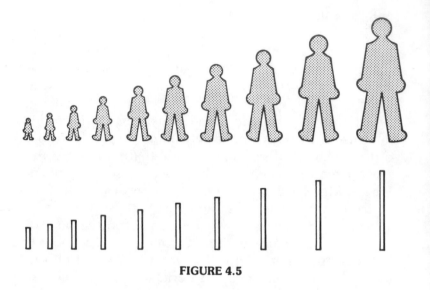

FIGURE 4.5

spreads the sticks apart so that corresponding elements of the two series are no longer opposite each other, points to one of the dolls, and asks, "Which stick will this one take?"[7]

The third kind of correspondence (cardinal) is tested by a second experiment.

Experiment II: Flowers and Vases
The subject is presented with several vases arranged in a neat row and a larger number of flowers in a bunch. He is asked to arrange the flowers "one flower for each vase, as many vases as flowers," but again, when the child succeeds in doing that (and confirms his success by inserting one flower into each vase), the experimenter, having discarded the extra flowers, spreads out or compresses one of the sets so that the corresponding elements of the two series are no longer opposite each

other. Then he asks the child whether there is "still the same number" in both sets.[8]

The terms *serial* and *ordinal* both refer to systematic asymetrical relations (for example, "Each element in this series is larger than the preceding and smaller than the following one," or "This element has the same ordinal position in this series as that one has in a different series"). The word *cardinal* refers to "how many" (for example, "There are as many elements in this set as there are in that one"). We shall compare Preoperational with Concrete Operational reactions to each of the experiments described earlier.

Preoperational

Early in the Preoperational Period, a child faced with the dolls-and-sticks problem fails to make even a semblance of a correct response. He fails to match the two series because he cannot arrange either one by itself into the proper order, and he cannot arrange any series in order because he lacks the structure that requires each element to be larger than the one preceding and smaller than the one following it (or vice versa).* Given a ran-

---

*That structure, once it *has* developed, leads to the operation known as *transitivity*. A child is said to be capable of transitivity when he understands that

if

  C is larger than B, and
  B is larger than A,

then

  C is larger than A.

domized series *A* through *J*, he may fail to impose *any* order on the display. Later, he may separate the elements (say the sticks) into "little" ones and "big" ones, without comprehending even the relation of "bigger" and "smaller," let alone the dual relation of "bigger than *X* and smaller than *Y*."[9]; or he may place the tops of the sticks in order from low to high but fail to take the bottoms into account. See Figure 4.6.

Once the seriation (placing in order) of a single set of objects is accomplished, one-to-one correspondence across sets (smallest-to-smallest, largest-to-largest, and similarly in between) becomes possible. Actually, however, rather than the seriation of a single set being a *prerequisite* to serial correspondence between two series, Piaget conceives of them as "the same thing." This is so

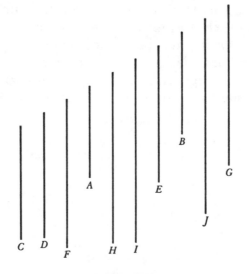

FIGURE 4.6

because not only does correspondence "presuppose seriation," but seriation "implies a kind of correspondence"[10]—presumably the relation of each element to the ones preceding and following it in the series.* *Seriation,* then, is an intrinsic correspondence (within a series) and *"serial correspondence"* is an extrinsic correspondence (between two or more series).

The correspondence is not *operational,* however, and it is therefore unstable. When one of the sets (say, the sticks) is spread apart so as to break up the perceptual correspondence (so that each stick is no larger immediately below the corresponding doll), the child is again confused. He is likely to choose the nearest stick for each doll (thereby leaving some dolls without sticks) rather than to seek out "the smallest," "next-to-the-smallest," and so on. He is unable to *reverse* his thinking back to the previous condition of obvious correspondence, he *centers* instead on the present physical proximity of elements, and he fails to take account of the *transformation* from the one to the other.

A similar difficulty shows up on the flowers-and-vases problem (which, you will recall, is designed to test *cardinal correspondence).* Early in the Preoperational Period, the child cannot even arrange the flowers in a one-to-one relation with the vases. He may set two lines of equal length, using all of the flowers, and then be surprised to have some flowers left over, once when he has actually inserted a flower into each vase.

Later, when he is able to establish the one-to-one correspondence by himself, he may be fooled if the exper-

---

*If this seems to you to require a very broad definition of *correspondence,* you are not alone. I, for one, am with you.

imenter then arranges one set of objects (the vases) in a line and the other set (the flowers) in a cluster; he no longer perceives the number of flowers to be equal to that of the vases, even if each flower is taken directly from a vase just before the rearrangement.

In terms of the "limitations of the Preoperational child" listed on p. 81, this performance would seem to involve at least *centering, states versus transformation, irreversibility,* and *transductive reasoning.* And all of those may be conceived in terms of classes-and-relations structure (see Figure 4.7). The row of flowers can be classified as smaller than, the same as, or larger than the row of vases. But that can be done on any of three dimensions: number, length, or density. Apparently what happens is that the subject fastens on the length dimension to the row of flowers *(centering, states versus transformation)* and fails to return to the representation of "same number" *(irreversibility, transductive reasoning).*

The child of this age lacks the classes-and-relations structure; and until he has that, those "limitations" will recur.

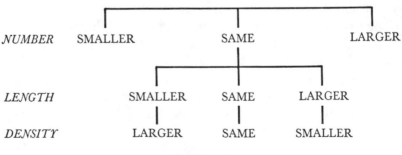

FIGURE 4.7

Concrete Operational

Whereas serial correspondence is said to be preoperational and qualitative ("intuitive"), *ordinal correspondence* is said to be operational and quantitative. The difference is both subtle and important.

In the dolls-and-sticks problem, operational thinking is not overwhelmed by that perceptual nearness of elements in two series; it can comprehend the order of elements in both series regardless of their physical proximity. The Concrete Operational child confidently picks out the right stick for each doll when one series is elongated with respect to the other, or even when one series is reversed. The child *decenters* from the physical proximity that had previously dominated his thought (the concepts "first," "second," "third," and so on now generalized to *any* succession of units, regardless of where they are or even what they are), and he can mentally *reverse* any deformation introduced by the experimenter. He *conserves ordinal correspondence.*

In the flowers-and-vases problem, the child in this period not only arranges the display correctly but is certain that he is correct, and he cannot be fooled by the experimenter's elongating one of the sets or gathering it into a cluster. When asked why he answers as he does, he says something like "They came out of the vases, so they'll go back into them" or "These are stretched out more, but there's just as many of those." The decentering and reversal processes are again effective, and the equivalence of sets is permanent: The child *conserves cardinal correspondence.*

It must be obvious to you now that the independence of numerosity from perceptual position effects is vital to the notion of number. What may not be so obvious is that numerosity is the "extension of a class" (p. 101) and that classifying and ordering are both involved in numbering. *Class inclusion* is involved in the sense that two is included in three, three is included in four, and so on. But number also requires relations of *order*. What happens in its construction is something like this:

1. All of the elements of a class (for example, the dolls, the sticks, the flowers, or the vases in a Piagetian test) are equivalent by definition with respect to the intension of that class. (They are all dolls, all sticks, or whatever.)
2. But, says Piaget, how is the child to distinguish one element from all others if (a) as just indicated, one of its properties (the class intension) does not differentiate it from other elements, and (b) all other properties (size, weight, color, and so on in the examples cited earlier) are ignored?
3. The answer is that he must introduce some kind of *order*. He may arrange them one after the other in space* or in time, but he *must* order them, for that is "the only way in which elements, which are otherwise being considered as identical, can be distinguished from one another.[11]

Number then, "is a synthesis of *class inclusion* and *relationships of order*."[12]

---

*This is not the "perceptual position effect" that cripples the thinking of the Preoperational child. Here the elements can be anywhere, just as long as they are in a row.

Conservation of Substance, Weight, and Volume: The Construction of Physical Quantity

Other problems are used to assess conservation of substance, weight, and volume. The term *conservation* refers to the subject's realization that certain properties (in this section, quantities of material) of a system remain the same in spite of transformations (of length and width) performed within the system. The meaning of the term *quantity* in common speech is clear only in context; the same is true here. In this section, when the term "quantity of substance" (or simply *substance*) is used, it refers to the amount of space occupied by the object, as judged by the child while he is looking at the object and only at the object; later, that same occupied space will be inferred from the amount of water displaced by the object and will be called *volume*. *Weight* is what might be expected—namely, the effect that the object has on the movement of a balance. The plasticene-balls problem (p. 86) and the two water-level problems (pp. 30 and 87) are examples of conservation of quantity. Let us first review the reaction of the Preoperational child to the plasticene-balls problem and then compare it with that of the child in the Concrete Operations Period.

Preoperational

One very important characteristic of the conservational structure is *reversibility* (see p. 84). Notice in Figure 4.8 that the third-order classification (width) is not a mere duplicate of the first and second (quantity and length); its freedom is restricted. If the quantity is the same (the special condition of conservation) and the length is smaller, the width cannot be smaller, same, or larger; it

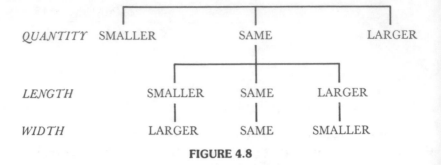

QUANTITY	SMALLER	SAME	LARGER
LENGTH	SMALLER	SAME	LARGER
WIDTH	LARGER	SAME	SMALLER

FIGURE 4.8

can only be larger. Similarly, if the length is larger, the width can only be smaller. This feature of conservation is called compensation by *reciprocity*. It is one of two kinds of reversibility; the other is compensation by *inversion* (sometimes called *negation*), or thinking one's way back to the original state of the display—in this example, to two balls of equal size. Piaget says that reciprocity consists of "modifications of the scheme to accommodate it to the initially disturbing element," whereas inversion cancels the disturbance.[13]

The Preoperational child cannot conserve at all. If the experimenter rolls the ball into a sausage right before the subject's eyes, the child will say that it becomes larger (or sometimes smaller) than the comparison ball. Refer to the list of limitations on page 81 for the reasons. Again, *centering, states versus transformation, irreversibility,* and *transductive reasoning* seem especially appropriate. And all of those limitations may be conceived as a lack of mobility within a classes-and-relations structure.

The "sausage" can be classified as smaller than, the same as, or greater than the ball. But that classification can be done on at least three bases: quantity, length, and width. (Depth, an obvious fourth one, will be omitted for the sake of simplicity.)

Figure 4.8 shows those relations. Remember that it represents a structure that the Preoperational child has not yet developed. He cannot move easily from one to another part of the figure in accordance with the rules implicit in it (always follow the lines). Instead, he centers on one dimension (length or width) and on the end-state rather than the transformation—an end-state that he blithely transfers from one dimension to another. Furthermore, he is committed to that end-state; he cannot mentally reverse the transformation and arrive back at "same quantity," either by using the gain in width to compensate for the loss in height (reciprocity) or by mentally undoing both (inversion). Surely reversibility must make an important contribution to the autonomy of central processes that was discussed in Chapter 1. Without such autonomy, children are dominated by their perceptions.

Concrete Operations

When he *can* do all of these things, he has moved into the Concrete Operations Period. At about the age of seven, he conserves substance but denies that the weight remains the same when a plasticene ball is molded into a sausage. Later (at around nine years of age), he conserves weight but not volume.* Each acquisition repre-

---

*It is not until he enters the Formal Operatons Period, at around eleven or twelve years of age, that he is able to conserve volume. That is, if you immerse that now-familiar plasticene pair, the ball and the sausage, in equal amounts of water held in twin beakers, he can tell by the level of the water that the two immersed objects are equal. This achievement apparently awaits the development of an integrated system of spatial coordinates such that a part of a given volume can be "used up" by an object, so that any material that had previously occupied that space must be displaced by an amount equal to the volume of the object. That requires a somewhat more complicated cognitive structure than knowing that a piece of plasticene is still the same size after it has been altered in shape.

sents for its own critical attribute—whether that is substance, weight, volume, or some other—an invariance similar to the one that the child achieved in his Sensorimotor Period when he constructed the scheme of the permanent object. Together, they give his world a stability that it has never had before.

Egocentrism and Decentering in the Representation of Objects

As was noted in Chapter 3, the Preoperational child has a well-developed representational ability. But there are still significant limitations on that ability. One such limitation is the inability to imagine an object from the perspective of another person. Piaget and Inhelder[14] have devised a simple test of this called the three-mountain problem (see Figure 4.9).[15] They set three "mountains" on a table and one chair at each side of the table. The child sits in one of the chairs, and a doll is moved from one to another of the three remaining chairs. Then the subject is asked what the doll sees from each of its three stations. He may respond by drawing a doll's-eye view from each position, by selecting from drawings already made, or by constructing the doll's view with cardboard cutouts.

Preoperational

The Preoperational child simply cannot do this at all.

Concrete Operations

In the early part of the Concrete Operations Period, some transformations are made correctly, but perform-

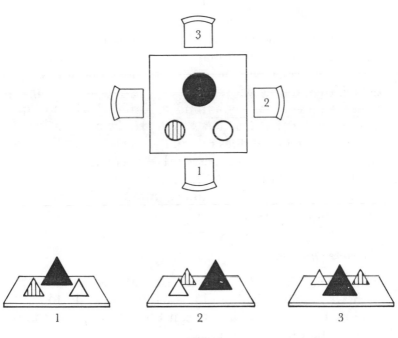

FIGURE 4.9

ance is extremely erratic. It is only in the latter half of the period that the child can identify the doll's view with confidence and accuracy.

Egocentrism and Decentering in Social Relations

Related to the child's ability to take another person's point of view toward a physical display are certain naturalistic observations of children in social situations—notably, situations in which they interact with each other.

Preoperational

There is a strong tendency, in such situations, for children in the Preoperational Period to engage either in *simple monologues,* which conform to the content of their own individual activities, or in *collective monologues,* in which Child *A* says something to Child *B* with no apparent intent that Child *B* should reply, or even hear; whereupon Child *B* does not, in fact, give any indication that he has heard, and responds by saying something totally unrelated to what Child *A* has just said.

They are incapable of intercommunication because neither of them is capable of taking the role of the other.

Concrete Operations

The development of concrete operations, with its increased mobility of thought, permits the child to shift rapidly back and forth between his own viewpoint and that of the other person.

It also makes possible the sharing of goals and the recognition of mutual responsibilities in the attainment of shared goals. In short, it makes cooperation possible.

"Cooperation" is "co-operation"—a coordination of operations. It is at about this time (age seven) that children begin to be interested in games with rules. In order to play such a game, one must be able to conceptualize the roles of the other players, and in fact children do develop that interest at the very same time that they begin to show in other ways their emancipation from egocentricity.*

---

*They find it difficult, however, to empathize with any younger child who spoils their game because he lacks this ability to conceptualize the interrelationship of roles.

Egocentrism and Decentering in Reasoning

Social interaction, however, has implications beyond itself—notably in the development of logical reasoning. For "reasoning is always a demonstration,"[16] and until the child is aware of a *need* for demonstration, he makes little progress toward developing that ability. Merely interacting freely with his physical environment results in some awareness of gaps and inconsistencies in his thinking, but what really brings them into focus is the difficulties that arise when he attempts to communicate his thoughts to others.

Piaget has done a series of studies on judgment and reasoning. One kind of study consists of a careful observation of children's spontaneous talking; another sets some task for them and then observes their reactions. Results from both kinds of study are essentially the same.

An interesting investigation of the latter kind concerns the conjunction *because*. There are three model uses of *because* that are legitimate expressions of relations between adjacent clauses:

1. *Causal explanation* establishes a cause-and-effect relation betwen two facts. ("He slipped because the pavement was icy.")

2. *Psychological* (or "motivational") explanation establishes a cause-and-effect relation between an intention and an act. ("I hit him because he took my candy." In this case, the intention is implied. Taking candy is not the proximate cause of being hit; anger and aggressive intent intervene.)

3. *Logical implication* establishes a reason-and-consequence relation between two ideas or two judgments. ("[I know] that animal is not dead because it is still moving.")[17]

Preoperational

The young child fails to discriminate among the three kinds of relations. In fact, within the causal mode, he often cannot even discriminate between a cause and its effect. Here are some responses to uncompleted sentences:

> I've lost my pen because *I'm not writing.*
> The man fell from his bicycle because *he broke his arm.*
> I teased that dog because *he bit me.*[18]

The "because" in each of these cases could be replaced by "and" or "in such a manner that." It is not a causal, a logical, or even a psychological relation; rather, it is a "consecutive" relation. The child does not use it consistently, however, even in that way; instead, he employs consecutive narrations, causal and psychological explanations, and even logical implications indiscriminately.*

---

*In a more free-form situation that the incomplete-sentence task, the confusions between causal and psychological explanations are so frequent that Piaget has found it useful to classify them into subcategories. One such category is *animism*—so called because the child imputes life to inanimate objects. In one demonstration, for example, he hung a metal box by two strings that were twisted in such a way that they would rotate the box as its weight pulled them out straight. The box was then released, and the subject was questioned about its spinning. The following dialogue is eloquent testimony to the young child's tendency to give psychological explanations of physical events:

> Why does it turn? *Because the string is twisted.*
> Why does the string turn too? *Because it wants to unwind itself.*
> Does the string know it is twisted? *Yes.*
> Why? *Because it wants to untwist itself. It knows it's twisted.*[19]

He has a foggy impression that two clauses belong together, and he uses "because" to make the connection; but he does not concern himself with the question of what *kind* of a relationship it is. His thinking consists of a mere *juxtaposition* of facts or ideas.

He really doesn't care about such distinctions, for in his egocentrism he believes that everyone thinks just as he does and therefore that he will be perfectly understood when he expresses his thoughts. He will experience many attempted communications between himself and others before that belief will change.

Concrete Operations

It seems paradoxical that egocentrism is overcome by becoming self-conscious, but that's the way it happens. Even as sensorimotor egocentrism was overcome when the infant became aware of himself as an object among other objects, so the older child has overcome his egocentrism when he can see himself as a thinker among other thinkers. And even as that change in the sensorimotor infant comes about as a result of interaction with those other objects, so the analogous change occurs in the older child as a result of interaction with those other thinkers.

By the age of seven or eight, the average child makes a distinction between psychological and causal explanations; but he still has trouble with logical implication and often reverts to psychological explanation in its stead. ("Half of 6 is 3 because *it's right*."[20] Eventually, at about the age of nine, he produces a full-fledged logical justification. ("Half of 6 is 3 because 3 plus 3 is 6.")

That performance is possible because the child is now capable of imposing direction and order on his thinking—a direction and order that he has found useful in communicating with others. "Only by means of friction against other minds," says Piaget, "by means of exchange and opposition does thought come to be conscious of its own aims and tendencies, and only in this way is it obliged to relate what could till then remain juxtaposed."[21]

Spatial Relations

We have noted that even the simplest of object perceptions is built up over a long period of time. It should not be surprising to find that development of an extensive system of spatial coordinates takes even longer.

It shouldn't be, but it is! Here is a demonstration: A child is presented with a glass bottle one-fourth filled with colored water and another (or an outline drawing thereof) just like it, but without the water. The second bottle is tipped off the vertical, and the subject is asked to indicate where its waterline would be if the water from the first bottle were poured into it.[22]

Preoperational

In the latter part of the Preoperational Period, the child centers on the configuration of the bottle, and the waterline is drawn with reference to that only (Figure 4.10).

Concrete Operations

The early part of the Concrete Operations Period is a transitional stage in which there is a conflict between taking reference cues from the bottle and using the

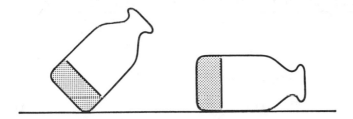

FIGURE 4.10

more stable horizontal and vertical contours of the sur-round (Figure 4.11). It is not until the child is nine or ten years old that he is able to give the correct response consistently (Figure 4.12).

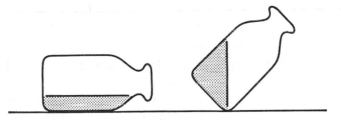

FIGURE 4.11

To me, the striking thing about all this is that the Euclidean space that we all take for granted not only is constructed rather than given but is also constructed over a period that covers most of a person's growing years.

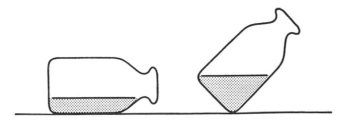

FIGURE 4.12

Distance, Time, Movement, and Velocity

Another such construction is that of *time*.[23] Children's answers to questions about time are often mildly surprising to adults, but when observations are made in situations deliberately contrived to illuminate the salient features of their thinking, the results are sometimes downright astonishing!

If the experimenter moves one object *(A)* from *a* to *d* and simultaneously moves another object *(B)* from *a* to *b* (Fig. 4.13), the early Preoperational child will insist that *A* "took longer" than *B*. Even more surprising is his response when the *B* object is moved twice (Fig. 4.14). The child may still maintain that *A* took longer than *B*!

He may say that *A* took longer because it is ahead of *B* or that *B* took a shorter time because it didn't have so far to go. In either case, he is centering on the spatial characteristics of the event and more particularly on

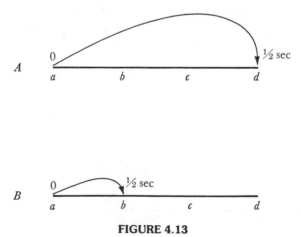

FIGURE 4.13

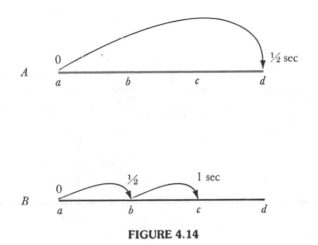

FIGURE 4.14

spatial *states* (as opposed to transformations); whereas movement (distance), velocity, and time in an adult are all differentiated parts of a single cognitive structure. That structure begins to form in the Preoperational Period, but it is thoroughly dominated by spatial perceptions.

In order to have a conception of time, it is necessary to develop conceptions of movement and velocity. But in order to have a conception of velocity, for example, it is necessary to develop a conception of time. It looks like a vicious circle; but before we give up, let's take a closer look at the child's conception of velocity.

Velocity is a relation between time and movement. We have seen how the young child deals with time; now let's test his conception of movement—the spatial displacement of an object in his visual field. The child is told that the two lines in Figure 4.15 are streetcar tracks, and that any small objects moved along them are streetcars.

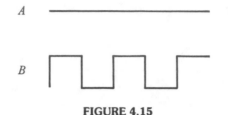

FIGURE 4.15

The experimenter moves a "car" over a given number of segments of Track *B* and asks the child to make a trip of the same length on *A* with his car. Since the movement is over a *distance,* this is a test of the *conservation of length* (distance).*

The child probably will move his car to a position opposite that of the experimenter, which of course means that his trip has actually been less than half as long. The early Preoperational child will continue to respond in this way even when supplied with a piece of cardboard—a potential measuring device—exactly equal in length to a segment of Track *B*.

This performance seems to have one characteristic in common with that of the time problem presented earlier. In both, there apparently is a centering on terminal spatial order—that is, given simultaneous starts from identical points on the spatial dimension "left-to-right," the child's answer depends on which car is farther to the right at the end of the episode.

We suspect, then, that centering on terminal position

---

*The most common method of testing for conservation of length is to display horizontally two sticks that the child recognizes as the same length, then to move one of them slightly to the right and ask him whether they are still the same length.

is at least a part of the problem—a hypothesis that can be applied to *velocity* problems.

In Figure 4.16, *A* represents the route of one object, *B* that of another; the Roman numerals indicate different problems, each of which takes but a few seconds to administer. In each of the four problems, the two objects start simultaneously and stop simultaneously. It is therefore obvious to an adult that in each problem, the velocity of Object *A* is greater than that of Object *B*.

But here are the responses of a subject in the Preoperational Subperiod:

In Problem I, the child says that "*A* and *B* travel at the same speed,"
 which they don't.
In Problem II, he says that "*A* is faster than *B*,"
 which, of course, is correct.

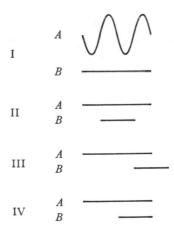

FIGURE 4.16

In Problem III, he says that "*B* is faster than *A*,"
which it is not.

In Problem IV, he believes that "*A* is faster,"
which, like his response to Problem II, is correct.

Thus II and IV are correct; I and III are not, since *A* is in fact faster than *B* in all four problems.

However, the interesting question in each case is, "Why?" All but one of those performances confirm the "terminal position" hypothesis. In I, II, and III, terminal position and perceived speed agree precisely, whereas in IV the hypothesis calls for a "same speed" response, and that is not what happens.

A slight variation in the experimental procedure gives us a clue to the reason for that exception. In this version of Problem IV, the objects move through tunnels from their initial to their final positions. When that is done, the child does say that they move at the same speed; and that, of course, is in line with the "terminal position" hypothesis.

But why should the addition of the tunnel have such an effect? Apparently there is another structure, "the passing scheme," that dominates over terminal position when the two are in conflict. The "passing scheme" is activated whenever one object is seen to overtake another (even if the action stops before an actual passing occurs). What the tunnel does is to prevent that structure from operating, so that the child then falls back onto his terminal position scheme.

Thus, although centering on terminal position is not what determines the response in all of the examples we have discussed here, there does seem to be a kind of *centering* that limits the competence of the Preoperational child in each one: and with the single exception of the "passing scheme," that centering is on an *end state* rather than a *transformation*.

Shifting back to time for a moment, we find centering again when we ask a young child how old someone is compared to someone else. His reply will depend entirely on the heights of the two persons judged. It might be regarded as a sort of "vertical terminal position" effect!

On page 127, we encountered a vicious circle in which the development of each of three concepts,

time	$(t = d/v)$
movement	$(d = vt)$
velocity	$(v = d/t)$

depends on the development of each of the others. Have we broken out of that circle? I'm not sure that we have. As a matter of fact, the physicists themselves have had trouble with this one, though Piaget suggests that a breakthrough may be in the making. A French physicist has proposed that velocity be defined in terms of the notion of passing—which is one way in which the Preoperational child "defines" it![24]

Properties of Groups and Groupings

The rules of mathematics and logic are widely used by psychologists to govern their own behavior as scientists, but Piaget uses them as models of the mental functioning of children. He is convinced that the rules of logic have developed, both phylogenetically and ontogenetically, as a result of the exigencies of living in a lawful universe. The actions that were first overt and then internalized now begin to form tightly organized *systems* of actions. Any internal act that forms an integral part of one of those systems Piaget calls an "operation." "Preoperational," "concrete operational," and "formal operational" describe different levels of systematic mental activity.

The actions implied by the following mathematical symbols are all examples of operations.[25]

+ combining	÷ dividing
− separating	> placing in order
× repeating	= possible substitution

These have their counterparts in logic; for example, "and" represents the action of *combining*; "except" represents the action of *separating*. Thus the structures of logic may be used to represent the structures of thought; the one serves as a model for the other.

That does not mean that people always think that way, but Piaget believes that any subject who ever thinks that way has a cognitive structure that can be represented in logical terms. Any other kind of thinking is regarded as a failure either to use a developed structure or to develop the structure in the first place.

In the Concrete Operations Period, structures often take the form that Piaget calls "groupings." A grouping is a system of operations that combines attributes of both the *group* and the *lattice*.[26]

The Group

A group is a system that consists of a set of elements and an operation on those elements such that the following principles apply:

Composition*

The result of every operation (remember that an operation is an action that is part of a system of actions) is itself a part of the system.† For example, if

$A \circ B = C,$

then C is a part of the system as well as A and B.

Associativity

When the operation is performed within the system,

$A \circ (B \circ C)$ is the same as
$(A \circ B) \circ C;$

then combining A with the result of combining B and C is the same as combining C with the result of combining A and B.

Identity

In every system there is one and only one element that, when combined with other elements in the system, leaves the result unchanged. It is called the *identity element*.

$A \circ I = A$, and
$I \circ A = A,$

where I is the identity element.
For example:

If the operation were addition, I would be 0;
if it were multiplication, I would be 1.

---

*Sometimes called *closure* or *combinativity*.

†The symbol ∘ here represents the operation. Addition and multiplication of integers are examples.

Reversibility

For every element, there is another that negates it. The negating element, called an *inverse,* is the only one that, when combined with the first element, yields the identity element.

$A \circ A' = I,$

where A' is the inverse of A.

> If the operation were addition, the inverse would be $(-A)$;
> if it were multiplication, the inverse would be $(1/A)$.

Here is a set of elements:

1 2 3 4 5 6 7 8 9

Let us say that the operation is addition. Is this set a group? The way to find out is to check it against the four properties just described, namely:

> *Composition:* The product (sum) of 8 and 9, for example, is 17, which is not within the system.
> *Associativity:* $(2 + 4) + (6 + 8) = 2 + (4 + 6) + 8 = 2 + 4 + (6 + 8)$, or any other example you may choose.
> *Identity:* There is no identity element in the set.
> *Reversibility:* There is no inverse.

The set meets only one of the criteria; it is not a group unless it meets all four.* What if the set were changed to include all positive and negative integers plus zero?

> *Composition:* The sum of any two or more integers yields an integer. $3 + 5 + 9 = 17$.

---

*It is a lattice, however. See pp. 137–139.

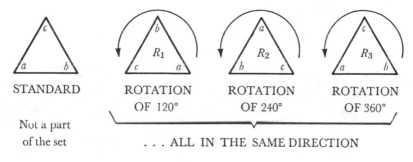

FIGURE 4.17

Associativity: It matters not whether the sum of 3 and 5 is added to 9 or 3 is added to the sum of 5 and 9.

Identity: Adding zero doesn't change anything.

Reversibility: For each positive integer, there is a negative that cancels it. $3 + (-3) = 0$.

This one does have all the properties of a group.*

It should perhaps be mentioned that even sensori-motor equilibrium can involve group structure. If each of the corners of the triangular block in Figure 4.17 were perceptually distinctive, a two-year-old child would be able to keep track of his own displacements of the object, including rotary ones. Those displacements would form a sensorimotor (sometimes called "practical") group. When a subject can *predict* the positions that will result from various relations, his cognition is said to be *operational*. If a Concrete Operational subject is predicting the positions of the block in Figure 4.17, his thinking will exhibit the following qualities:

---

*It also has all properties of a lattice.

Composition

The product of any two or more of the possible rotations is also one of them.

$$R_1 \circ R_1 = R_2$$
$$R_1 \circ R_2 = R_3$$
$$R_1 \circ R_3 = R_1$$

Associativity

Given a specific set of rotations, it does not matter in what combination the operations are performed.

$$(R_2 \circ R_2) \circ R_1 = R_1 \circ R_1 = R_2$$
$$R_2 \circ (R_2 \circ R_1) = R_2 \circ R_3 = R_2$$

Identity

Because R_3 returns to its point of origin, it is the identity element in the set.

Reversibility

R_1 is the inverse of R_2 and vice versa, because their resultant is R_3, the identity element.

The Sensorimotor group is a model of the structure of *overt actions;* the Formal Operations group is concerned with propositions, as described in Chapter 5 (although the mathematical modeling of formal thought is too intricate to be treated adequately in a text of this kind, and no attempt will be made to do so); the Concrete Operational group combines with the lattice to model the qualities of thinking that are of primary concern in this chapter.

The Lattice

A lattice is a structure consisting of a set of elements and a relation that can encompass two or more of those elements. Specifically, that relation must be such that any two elements have one *least upper bound* (l.u.b.) and one *greatest lower bound* (g.l.b.). The least upper bound of two elements is the smallest element that includes them both. If Element *B* includes Element *A* and some other element(s), then the l.u.b. of *A* and *B* is *B*. In a hierarchy of classes, for example if Class *B* includes *A* as a subclass, the l.u.b. of *A* and *B* is *B* (see Figure 4.18). Similarly, the greatest lower bound is the largest element that is included in both. Since *A* is included both in itself and in *B*, but *B* is included in itself only, the g.l.b. of *A* and *B* is *A*.

Here is a set of elements:

1 2 3 4 5 6 7 8 9

Again, the operation is addition. Is the set a lattice? Take 5 and 8, for example:

8 is the smallest element that includes both (l.u.b.), and
5 is the largest element that is included in both (g.l.b.).

Figure 4.19 shows another set of elements, this one arranged in a class hierarchy. Can you find an l.u.b. and a g.l.b. for any pair of these elements?

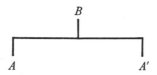

FIGURE 4.18

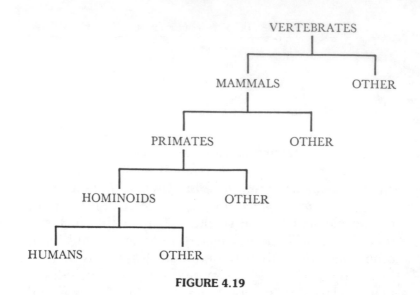

FIGURE 4.19

Take the pair "vertebrate-mammal," for example:

Vertebrate is the smallest class that includes both classes, and *mammal* is the largest class that is included in both.

Other possible two-element relations are mammal-primate, primate-hominoid, and hominoid-human. Since in any one of those it is possible to find both an l.u.b. and a g.l.b., this hierarchy is therefore a lattice. As a matter of fact, the lattice seems to be a particularly useful device for representing logical classes and relations in hierarchical form,* although it also is used to model the so-called combinatorial analysis of formal thought, in which the outcomes are propositions or statements of

---

*Piaget himself uses a hierarchy of classes to illustrate the properties of a lattice. It might better be called a "quasi-lattice," however; because although all the vertical relations in the diagrams (*A*, *B*, and *C*, and so on) meet the requirements of a lattice, the horizontal ones (*A* and *A'*, *B* and *B'*, *C* and *C'*, and so on) do not. The members of a horizontal pair are exclusive classes by definition.

possibilities rather than the tangible realities that concern the Concrete Operational child. It should be noted in this regard that to qualify as models of concrete operations, the contents processed by each structure must be just that—concrete. Later on, the adolescent will be able to formulate an abstract definition of, say, a "mammal" or a "primate"; but at this stage the child works with concrete exemplars of each class.

The Grouping

We have now had a brief look at the properties of *groups* and of *lattices*. *Groupings* include aspects of them both. Nine distinct groupings make their appearance during the Concrete Operations Period. Describing them all would be beyond the scope of this book, but fortunately the first one ("Grouping I") illustrates the basic characteristics of all of them. Grouping I (Figure 4.20), Primary Addition of Classes, is concerned with class hierarchies of the form $A + A' = B$, $B + B' = C$, and so on, where A is an independently defined category and

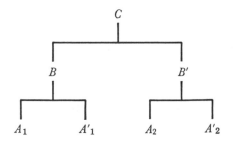

FIGURE 4.20

A' comprises "all the B that is not A." For example, if A were "humans" and B were "humanoids," A' would be "chimpanzees, gibbons, gorillas, and orangutans." *Posing* ("setting up" or "thinking of") a class is logical *addition;* *unposing* ("excluding" or "omitting") is *subtraction.* The nature of the hierarchy becomes apparent when we add two subordinate classes:

Posing both A and A' is the equivalent of posing B.
Posing B and B' together is the same as posing C.

Conversely,

$B - A = A'$, and $B - A - A' = 0$

Using the notation just presented, turn back to Figure 4.19 and note that if the class "humans" were designated as A, then "hominoids" would be B, "primates" C, "mammals" D, and "vertebrates" E.

Now try translating the preceding equations into the more concrete terms of the zoological classification:

$A + A' = B$, for example, becomes humans + anthropoid apes = all hominoids

$B + B' = C$ is now hominoids + monkeys, lemurs, and so on = all primates

$B - A = A'$ becomes hominoids − humans = anthropoid apes

$B - A - A' = 0$ is now hominoids − humans − anthropoid apes = an empty or null class

The grouping has, by virtue of its kinship with the group, a *general identity element,* which, as you will recall, "when combined with other elements in the system, leaves the result unchanged." But in addition to general identity, the grouping has, by virtue of its kinship to the lattice, a *special identity element*. The new element appears in two operations:

1. *Tautology:* $A + A = A$. (The class "humans" when combined with the class "humans" yields the class "humans.")
2. *Resorption:* $A + B = B$; $A + C = C$; and so on. (Humans combined with hominoids yields hominoids; humans combined with primates yields primates; and so on.)

The special identity element in each of these is A—in this example, the class "humans."

These are but a few of the many examples that could be given; many more could be generated by the single hierarchy depicted in Figure 4.19. They would all have characteristics of both group and lattice,* but Piaget believes that, for the most part, children's behavior is consonant with neither the group nor the lattice as such; so he has formulated a hybrid, the grouping, as a more adequate model of their thinking.

At this point, I am constrained to make a comment that may either anger or relieve the reader, depending on how meticulously he has worked to master the material so far presented. My comment is this: It is not the details of the system presented here that are important;

---

*But they would not have all those characteristics. When this class hierarchy was presented as a lattice (p. 138), I pointed out that it did not have all the properties thereof. The same must be said of it as a group, for $B - A - A'$ lacks associativity; $(B - A) - A' = 0$, but does $B - (A - A')$? Actually, A' cannot be subtracted from A at all, because the two are exclusive categories.

what is important is *the idea of system itself.* Piaget does not conceive of responses being connected to stimuli as the child develops, but rather of actions being related to other actions within a *system* of actions. In the Concrete Operations Period, any change in one part of that system has implications for other parts. This is true as well of the formal Operations Period, but the "parts" there are so varied and the systems so complex that I have chosen the earlier period to illustrate Piaget's use of logic as a model of thought. If you have found this section even a little difficult, you will be grateful for that decision. If not, there are other books that include more technical treatments of Formal Operations.[27]

Summary

Since birth, the dominant organizing activities of the child have changed from *overt actions* (in the Sensorimotor Period) to *perceptions and images* (in the Preoperational Period) to *intellectual operations* (in the Concrete Operations Period). Those operations occur within a framework of classes and relations that make possible what Piaget calls *mobility* of thinking—decentering, reversibility, taking the view of others, and so on. As a result, the Concrete Operational child conserves quantity and number, constructs the time and space that he will live with as an adult, and establishes foundations for the kind of thinking that is the identifying feature of the next and final period of his intellectual development.

In the introduction to this chapter, I posed a question about autonomy of thinking. Have you found an answer yet? If not, keep trying as you read Chapter 5, on Formal Operations.

Notes

1. Piaget and Inhelder, *The Child's Conception of Space* (1948 [1956]), p. 36.

2. Flavell, *The Developmental Psychology of Jean Piaget* (1963), p. 166.

3. Piaget, "The Theory of Stages in Cognitive Development" (1971), p. 2.

4. The primary source of the material in this section is Piaget and Inhelder, *La Genese des Structures Logiques Elementaire: Classifications et Seriations* (1959); the recommended reference in English is Flavell, *The Developmental Psychology of Jean Piaget* (1963).

5. This is similar to a problem first described in Piaget, *The Child's ption of Number* (1941 [1952]), p. 165. The quotations are paraphrased.

6. Piaget and Inhelder, *La Genese des Structures Logiques Elementaire*, (1959), pp. 55–56; as quoted by Flavell in his *The Developmental Psychology of Jean Piaget* (1963).

7. Piaget, *The Child's Conception of Number* (1941 [1952]), p. 97.

8. *Ibid.*, p. 49.

9. *Ibid.*, p. 99.

10. *Ibid.*, p. 102.

11. Piaget, *Genetic Epistemology* (1970), p. 38.

12. *Ibid.*, italics added.

13. Piaget, *The Development of Thought: Equilibration of Cognitive Structures* (1975 [1977]), p. 26.

14. Piaget and Inhelder, *The Child's Conception of Space* 1948 [1956]), p. 210.

15. Adapted from *ibid.*, p. 211.

16. Piaget, *Judgment and Reasoning in the Child* (1924 [1928]), p. 2.

17. *Ibid.*, p. 6.

18. Ibid., p. 17.

19. Piaget, *The Child's Conception of the World* (1926 [1929]), pp. 175–176.

20. Piaget, *Judgment and Reasoning in the Child* (1924 [1928]), p. 26.

21. *Ibid.*, pp. 11–12.

22. Adapted from Piaget and Inhelder, *The Child's Conception of Space* (1948 [1956]), p. 383.

23. A more detailed account of the experiments on time, measurement, and velocity is available in Chapter 9 of Flavell's *The Developmental Psychology of Jean Piaget* (1963), especially pp. 316–326.

24. Piaget, "The Child and Modern Physics" (1957), p. 51.

25. Flavell, *The Developmental Psychology of Jean Piaget* (1963), p. 166.

26. This discussion leans heavily on the synthesizing work of Flavell, *ibid.*, pp. 168 ff.

27. Inhelder and Piaget, *The Growth of Logical Thinking from Childhood to Adolescence* (1955 [1958]) is the standard source; a briefer treatment can be found in Ginsburg and Opper, *Piaget's Theory of Intellectual Development* (1979); and Flavell's *The Developmental Psychology of Jean Piaget* (1963) is intermediate between these two.

5

The Formal
Operations Period
(11–15 Years)

5

The Formal
Operations Period
(11–15 Years)

Marvelous though they are when compared, for example, to the most advanced thinking of any subhuman species, Concrete Operations still fall far short of the intellectual accomplishments of the most intelligent of human adults. My purpose in this chapter is not to analyze those adult accomplishments in great detail, but rather to identify the crucial characteristics that differentiate them from earlier ones. Consequently, the chapter is relatively brief.

Another reason for the relative brevity of this chapter is that the characteristics of adult thinking are somewhat more accessible than are the processes discussed earlier. Every college course is an enterprise that requires a great deal of thinking; one hopes that much of it is logical. A person who is looking for the *operations* involved in that thinking may be able to find some of them. A better way to focus attention on those operations would be to take a course in logic. Those students who can arrange to include such a course in their curriculum should do so, but should look at it from a psychological viewpoint, remembering always the Piagetian dictum that *logic* is the mirror of *thought*, rather than vice versa. That is, for him the function of logic is to make explicit those mental processes that occur naturally at the highest level of human development.

Before turning the reader over to a logician, however, there are a few general things that I wish to say about the transition from Concrete to Formal Operations. I shall describe but a single problem, so that its implications may be examined in reasonable detail.

Archimedes' Law of Floating Bodies

An object will float if its specific gravity is less than 1.00—that is, if its density is less than that of water. In an experimental test, this can be reduced to a comparison of the *weights of equal volumes* of the two substances. Some subjects are able to derive this law while being questioned by the investigator. But by no means are all of them competent to do so, and the differences among them are related to differences in age.

Apparatus
The subject is presented with
1. A bucket of water
2. Several different objects, each small enough to fit into the bucket
3. Three cubes of the same size but different densities

and an empty plastic cube, also of the same size, to facilitate comparisons of the density of other materials with that of water

Procedure
The subject is asked to classify the objects according to whether they will float and to explain the basis of his classification in each case. Then he is allowed to experiment with the materials and is asked to summarize his observations and to look for a *law* that will tie them all together.

Concrete Operations Applied to the Floating Bodies Problem

My purpose in this and the following two sections "Operations on Operations" and "The Real Versus the Possible is to analyze the behavior of school-age children and adolescents in the situation just described. I shall first present some examples of performances by subjects who are not yet in the Formal Operations Period.

Although the Preoperational child in this situation blithely invokes a special cause for each event, the Concrete Operational child is troubled by inconsistencies that had not concerned him earlier because they had not existed for him; he had lacked "instruments of coordination (operational classifications, and so on), which will attain equilibrium only at the point when concrete operations are structured."[1]

That equilibrium is not attained suddenly, but progress is made precisely because of the child's awareness that he is in difficulty. In the early part of the Concrete Operations Period, the main contradiction is that certain large objects will float and certain small ones sink. It is a contradiction because he begins the period with a kind of "absolute weight" concept as his main tool for dealing with the problem. Each object, including each bucket of water, has a "weight" that is conceived as a force that somehow opposes other forces, but in no consistent manner. (Remember that weight is not yet being conserved.) One moment he may predict that water will push a solid object up, the next moment that it will push one down. Initially, the only "weight" he knows is a property of each separate object, not of the substance of which the object is constituted; hence the term "absolute weight." Moreover, the child assigns a weight to an object by placing it on a scale something like that shown in Figure 5.1; size and weight are not discriminated as separate dimensions. That soon changes, however.

> BAR [seven years, eleven months] first classifies the bodies in three categories: those that float because they are light [wood, matches, paper, and the aluminum cover]; those that sink because they are heavy [large and small keys, pebbles of all sizes, ring clamps, needles and nails, a metal cylinder, and an eraser]; and those that remain suspended at a midway point [fish].
> "The needle?"
> "It goes down because it's iron."
> "And the key?"
> "It sinks too."

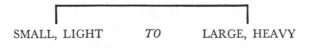

SMALL, LIGHT   *TO*   LARGE, HEAVY

FIGURE 5.1

"And the small things?" [nails, ring clamps]
"They are iron too."
"And this little pebble?"
"It's heavy because it's stone."
"And the little nail?"
"It's just a little heavy."
"And the cover, why does it stay up?"
"It has edges and sinks if it's filled with water."
"Why?"
"Because it's iron."[2]

One process that seems to be going on here is the assimilation of new objects into established categories of physical experience. The needle "goes down because it's iron"; the nails, ring clamps, and probably the key "are iron too." The pebble is "heavy because it's stone." Even the aluminum pan lid, which does not sink unless it is filled with water, is said to sink "because it's iron." The classification of some substances as light and others as heavy is a step toward the conception of density—the classification of substances according to their weights with volume held constant. That this child can*not* conceive density should not be surprising if you remember that neither of its two ingredients—weight and volume is yet being conserved.

Although it does not always show in the protocols, children early in the Concrete Operations period often make a three-way "sinkability" classification. Some objects can be relied on to float, others will surely sink, and still others may either float or sink, depending on the circumstances (for example, the aluminum pan lid just mentioned).

The foregoing example (BAR, age seven years, eleven months) demonstrates the Concrete Operational child's ability to classify objects; but it also reveals a notable lack of refinement of the relevant structures. What the child needs as a foundation for the impending "operations on operations" stage is a structure something like that shown in Figure 5.2, which relates the perceived space occupied by a body to its perceived weight. Does he have such a structure? Here is BAR again, thirteen months later:

BAR [nine years]. [Class 1] Floating objects: ball, pieces of wood, corks, and an aluminum plate. [Class 2] Sinking objects: keys, metal weights, needles, stones, large block of wood, and a piece of wax. [Class 3] Objects that may either float or sink: covers.

[Seeing] a needle at the bottom of the water [BAR] says: "Ah! They are too heavy for the water, so the water can't carry them."

"And the tokens?"

"I don't know; they are more likely to go under."

"Why do these things float?" [Class 1]

"Because they are quite light."

"And the covers?"

"They can go to the bottom because the water can come up over the top."

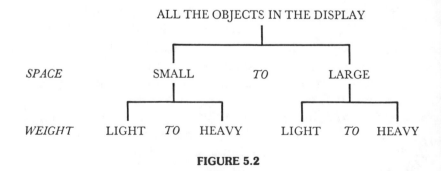

FIGURE 5.2

"And why do these things sink?" [Class 2]

"Because they are heavy."

"The big block of wood?"

"It will go under."

"Why?"

"There is too much water for it to stay up."

"And the needles?"

"They are lighter."

"So?"

"If the wood were the same size as the needle, it would be lighter."

"Put the candle in the water. Why does it stay up?"

"I don't know."

"And the cover?"

"It's iron; that's not too heavy, and there is enough water to carry it."

"And now?" [It sinks.]

"That's because the water got inside."

"And put the wooden block in."

"Ah! Because it's wood that is wide enough not to sink."

"If it were a cube?"

"I think that it would go under."

"And if you push it under?"

"I think it would come back up."

"And if you push this plate?" [aluminum]

"It would stay at the bottom."

"Why?"

"Because the water weights on the plate."

"Which is heavier, the plate or the wood?"

"The piece of wood."

"Then why does the plate stay at the bottom?"

"Because it's a little lighter than the wood; when there is water on top there is less resistance and it can stay down. The wood has resistance, and it comes back up."

"And this little piece of wood?"

"No, it will come back up because it is even lighter than the plate."

"And if we begin again with this large piece of wood in the smallest bucket, will the same thing happen?"

"No, it will come back up because the water isn't strong enough: there is not enough weight from the water [to hold down the wood]."[3]

I'm sure we can agree that BAR is pretty badly confused. He did, at one point near the beginning of the episode, hit on an idea that might have been expanded into a solution: He said, "If the wood were the same size as the needle, it would be lighter." Why did he fail to develop that point? He failed because he still lacks the structure delineated in Figure 5.2. Instead of using a general operational form in dealing with the relation of weight to occupied space, he is virtually limited to a particular case—the comparison of iron with wood. Moreover, when he does make comparisons, they are (with the single exception noted earlier) not comparisons of the weights of *equal amounts* of substances. The concept of specific gravity demands just such a comparison. But when BAR compares the weight of an object with that of water, he compares it with the entire quantity of water in the bucket: the same piece of wood will sink in one bucket, float in another.

Thus, bothered by vaguely perceived inadequacies in his explanations, BAR blunders energetically into one contradiction after another, until by the end of the session he has reverted to explanation by absolute weight.

It is a temporary regression, however. In general, the Concrete Operational child is much more orderly in his thinking than that. Even in the earlier session (seven years, eleven months) BAR classified the objects into three "sinkability" categories. And the third of those categories (objects that float or sink, depending on the circumstances) becomes further refined during the course of the period:

> RAY [nine years]: "The wood isn't the same as iron. It's lighter; there are holes in between."
> "And steel?"
> "It stays under because there aren't any holes in between."
>
> DUM [nine years, six months]: The wood floats "because there is air inside"; the key does not "because there isn't any air inside."[4]

"Float-or-sink-depending-on-the-circumstances" has become "more-or-less-filled," and that serves the child quite well in his quest for reduction of inconsistencies.

However, because "the water" is for him the volume of all the water in the container rather than just that displaced by the object, the ultimate explicit comparison between a measured volume of water and an equal volume of the other substances does not occur. Until he can understand the dynamics of displacement of liquids (until he can "conserve volume"), it *cannot* occur. The space dimension in Figure 5.2 must be replaced by volume, and the subject must realize that density varies directly with weight and inversely with volume. The revised structure is more difficult to diagram, but I have attempted it in Figure 5.3. (Notice that the space dimension in Figure 5.2 becomes the volume dimension here and is reversed in order to provide a single continuum of density at the bottom of the diagram.)

The adolescent who *has* developed that structure can think of displaced water as one of the objects in the display; all that is needed now to solve the floating bodies problem is an explicit comparison of *equal* volumes of (1) water and (2) the substance of the target object.

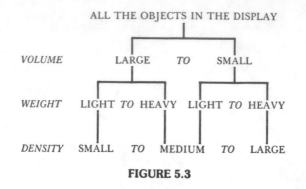

FIGURE 5.3

But since neither conservation of volume nor this elaborated structure becomes available until the Formal Operations Period, that solution is normally deferred until the subject is at least eleven years of age.

Operations on Operations

When weight and volume do at last become operational, the adolescent can place them in a logical relationship to each other—a relation known as *proportion:*

$$\frac{W}{V} = d$$

where

W is the weight* of a body
V is the volume of that body
d is its density

---

*A general formula would have to invoke the concept of *mass;* but in this situation weight is satisfactory because the force of gravity remains constant from one observation to another.

If we assume that an object is "solid," it will float if its "specific gravity" is less than 1.00—that is, if

$$\frac{d_o}{d_w} < 1$$

where

  d_o is the density of the object
  d_w is the density of water

The important thing to note about all this is that the adolescent is *operating on operations.* Piaget refers to *second-order operations,* and if my reading of him is correct, those operations constitute one of the fundamental characteristics of the Formal Operations Period. A Concrete Operational child knows that the product of replicating a given object 3 times is 3 (not counting the model, of course), and he knows that if that set of 3 is replicated 4 times, he'll have 12 of the objects. The adolescent has mastered those operations, but he can also place the resulting sets into relationship to each other: 12 is to 3 as 4 is to 1. To put it another way, 12/3 has the same *form* as 4/1. Before he can understand such a relationship, the adolescent must be able to *operate* formally *on* concrete *operations.*

In the Piagetian experiments, the concept of weight involves at least the operations of placing an object in a *series* of small to large gravity forces and of establishing a *correspondence* between that series and a series of inputs from the balance scale used to measure it. Moreover, the concept of volume requires similar, although more complex, operations, including the structuring of a correspondence between visual space and displacement of liquid. Those are operations with objects, and they are necessary to the solution of the floating bodies problem. They are *necessary*, but not *sufficient*. The adolescent starts with concrete operations; but then, in the floating bodies problem, he places them into a logical relationship to each other—a proportion $(W/V = d)$. Indeed, in order to educe the concept of "specific gravity," he must make a proportion out of two other proportions $(W_O/V_O$ and $W_W/V_W)$. In each case, he *operates on operations*.

The Real Versus the Possible

As he grows older and gains more experience, the child's construction of reality becomes more precise and extended, and that makes him aware of gaps in his understanding that had been masked by the vagueness of his previous constructions. He fills those gaps with *hypotheses*, and he is able to formulate—and often even to test—hypotheses without actually manipulating concrete objects. More accurately, he develops a new theoretical synthesis in which "certain relations are necessary,"[5] so that particular propositions can be checked, not only against the data of his senses (and against the data-bound mental operations of the previous period) but also against this new structure of *possibilities*. In fact, he *begins* by considering possibilities.

The following examples illustrate formal operations in the floating bodies problem:

> FRAN [twelve years, one month] does not manage to discover the law, but neither does he accept any of the earlier hypotheses. He classifies correctly the objects presented here but hesitates before the aluminum wire.
> "Why are you hesitating?"

"Because of the lightness, but no, that has no effect."
"Why?"
"The lightness has no effect. It depends on the sort of matter: for example, the wood can be heavy, and it floats." And for the cover: "I thought of the surface."
"The surface plays a role?"
"Maybe, the surface that touches the water, but that doesn't mean anything."
Thus he discards all of his hypotheses without finding a solution.

FIS [twelve years, six months] also . . . comes close to solution, saying in reference to a penny that it sinks "because it is small, it isn't stretched enough. . . . You would have to have something larger to stay at the surface, something of the same weight and which would have a greater extension."[6]

Observe the difference between these performances and those of the Concrete Operational child. Here there is a kind of transcendence of the immediate—a systematic trying out of possibilities. These subjects actually formulate hypotheses about the problem.

A child in the Concrete Operations Period does not formulate hypotheses, in the usual sense of imagining what events would occur under conditions that also are imagined. His accommodations are to events in the real world; he can only classify objects or events, place them in serial relationship to each other, and establish a correspondence of units in different categories. Tall dolls get tall sticks; greater movement of a spring balance means heavier weight; certain materials sink while others float; and so on. It is true that the ability to do these things implies a cognitive framework into which yet-to-be-experienced events can be placed (if, for example, he has built a structure in which $A < B < C$, he can extend the series to D, E, F, and so on, or if $A < C < E$ he may interpolate B and D); but the possible is always a limited and direct extension of concrete reality.

At the age of twelve, however, we find FRAN trying out *hypotheses* in his mind and discarding them as inappropriate, without any necessity of actually manipulating materials. FIS transforms the "more-or-less-filled" category of the Concrete Operations Period into a relationship between the weight-to-volume ratio of the object and the weight-to-volume ratio of water. And at age fourteen, another subject (WUR) actually manipulates one variable systematically while holding all others constant, which of course is the classical method of experimental science; but the experiments are designed to provide empirical tests of *possibilities* conceived *before* any manipulation.

The Preoperational child is capable of preposterous flights of fancy; the Concrete Operational child's thinking is limited by his concern for organizing the actual data of his senses. The adolescent in the Formal Operations Period is like both of those and different from each. He is capable of departures from reality, but those departures are lawful; he is concerned with reality, but reality is only a subset within a much larger set of possibilities.

Egocentrism

The introduction to "possibilities" has a curious side effect. The subject's thinking becomes *egocentric*. The term *egocentrism* is usually used by Piagetian scholars to refer to one outstanding characteristic of a child's thinking while he is in the Preoperational Period. In truth, however, Piaget says that egocentrism occurs not in just one period but in each of three periods.

The three major periods of development—Sensorimotor, Concrete Operations, and Formal Operations*—represent three different fields of cognitive action, and at the beginning of each there is a relative lack of structural differentiation and functional equilibrium. To the neonate, the world is his *actions* on it; to the Preoperational child, his own *representations* of the world of physical objects are the only ones possible. The adolescent's egocentrism results from the extension of his thinking into the realm of the *possible* through the instruments of propositional logic. He fails "to distinguish between the ego's new and unpredicted capacities and the social or cosmic universe to which they are applied."[8] He is drunk with possibilities, and he "forms theories about everything."[9] It is during this time that his own cerebration seems to him omnipotent, and it is then that he is likely to annoy his elders with all sorts of idealistic schemes designed to bring reality into line with his own thinking. He, too, is "egocentric."

"Formal" as Pertaining to "Form"

You should now be in a position to appreciate the significance of the title "Formal Operations." An example

---

*The Preoperational Period may be regarded as a preparation for Concrete Operations.

is the quantitative relationship cited earlier: "12 is to 3 as 4 is to 1." So too are the comprehension and appreciation of metaphor, of irony and satire, of proverbs and parables, of analogies of all kinds. Advanced mathematics and scientific constructs in many content areas are all results of formal thinking.

The adolescent can follow the form of an argument even if it means disregarding certain implications of its specific content. Younger children are not able to do that. If, for example, we present to a Concrete Operational child the following sentence:[10]

"I am very glad I do not [like] onions, for if I liked them, I would always be eating them, and I hate eating unpleasant things,"

he will respond to the *content* of the sentence by saying, in effect:

"Onions are unpleasant";
"it is wrong not to like them"; and so on.

The adolescent, on the other hand, will respond to the *form* of the argument by focusing on the contradiction between

"if I liked them" and
"onions are unpleasant."

Or take the syllogism

"All children like spinach";
"boys are children";
"therefore boys like spinach."

The younger child will respond to the content (particularly if he is a boy who doesn't like spinach!), but the adolescent can follow the argument* because he is impressed by its form.

This is the culmination of a trend that began when he emerged from the Sensorimotor Period: the dissociation of operative form and figurative content. In the beginning, you recall, his every scheme was the structure of overt actions on objects, so structure and content were inseparable. Now, as you can see, he is capable of dealing with the form of an argument without regard to its particular content.

Summary

Let us summarize what has been said about the Formal Operations Period. The adolescent begins where the Concrete Operational child left off—with *concrete operations*. He then *operates on those operations* by casting them into the form of propositions. The propositions then become part of a cognitive structure that owes its existence to past experience but makes possible hypotheses

---

*He can, but that doesn't mean that he necessarily does. Morgan and Morton presented *college* students with the following syllogism:

"Some ruthless men deserve a violent death. Since one of the most ruthless men was Heydrich, the Nazi hangman, therefore

1. Heydrich, the Nazi hangman, deserved a violent death.
2. Heydrich may have deserved a violent death.
3. Heydrich did not deserve a violent death.
4. None of these conclusions logically follows."[11]

Thirty-seven percent of the subjects chose number one!

Of course it is possible that those who did were still Concrete Operational even in college. Many college students are,[12] in spite of Piaget's norms (p. 45).

that do not correspond to any particular experience. The Concrete Operational child always starts with experience and makes limited interpolations and extrapolations from the data available to his senses. The adolescent, however, begins with the *possible* and then checks various possibilities against memorial representations of past experiences, and perhaps against sensory feedback from the concrete manipulations that are suggested by his hypotheses. A final reason that cognition is relatively independent of concrete reality is that the *content* of a problem has at last been subordinated to the *form* of relations within it.

So, from its sensorimotor origins, in which knowledge consisted of *actions* on the immediate environment, intelligence has moved through a period in which things are as they *appear* to be, through another in which they are as they *must* be, and finally to one in which knowledge includes not only a large set of stable concepts about the world, but a much larger set of inferences, deductions and implications that vastly extend the scope of consciousness.

Now have you resolved that paradox (pp. 99–100) about autonomy?

Chapter 1 was designed to serve as a summary as well as an introduction. Study it now as a summary.

Notes

1. Inhelder and Piaget, *The Growth of Logical Thinking from Childhood to Adolescence* (1955 [1958]), p. 28.

2. *Ibid.*, p. 29.

3. *Ibid.*, p. 33.

4. *Ibid.*, p. 35.

5. *Ibid.*, p. 251.

6. *Ibid.*, pp. 37–38.

7. *Ibid.*, p. 44.

8. *Ibid.*, p. 345.

9. Piaget, *The Psychology of Intelligence* (1947 [1950]), p. 148.

10. The example is a nonsense sentence by Ballard, quoted in Piaget's *Logic and Psychology* (1952 [1957]), p. 18. The first line of Piaget's quotation of Ballard actually reads, "I am very glad I do not *eat* onions" (italics mine). Since I was unable to find the original, I hope both the reader and Piaget will forgive the substitution of "like" for "eat." I am reasonably certain that the latter is an error of transcription.

11. Morgan and Morton, "The Distortion of Syllogistic Reasoning Produced by Personal Convictions" (1944), pp. 48–49.

12. McKinnon and Renner, "Are Colleges Concerned with Intellectual Development?" (1971), p. 1049.

Bibliography

This bibliography provides the original date of publication; where applicable, the date of the current edition used follows in brackets. This system allows the reader to scan dates of first appearance and hence of theoretical contributions in the order in which they were made.

Athey, I. J., and D. O. Rubadeau. 1970. *Educational Implications of Piaget's Theory.* Waltham, Mass.: Ginn-Blaisdell.

Ausubel, D. P. 1961. "Reception Versus Discovery Learning in Classroom Instruction," *Educational Theory,* 2: 21–24.

Baum, R. 1975. *Logic.* New York: Holt, Rinehart and Winston.

Beth, E. W., and J. Piaget. 1961 [1966]. *Mathematical Epistemology and Psychology.* Trans. W. Mays. New York: Gordon and Breach.

Birch, H. G. 1945. "The Relation of Previous Experience to Insightful Problem Solving." *Journal of Comparative Psychology,* 38: 367–383.

Bloom, B. S., J. Thomas Hastings, and G. F. Madaus. 1971. *Handbook on Formative and Summative Evaluation of Student Learning.* New York: McGraw-Hill.

Bower, T. G. R. 1966. "The Visual World of Infants." *Scientific American*, 215(6): 80–92. (Offprint 502.)

——— 1967. "Phenomenal Identity and Form Perception in an Infant." *Journal of Perception and Psychophysics*, 2: 74–76.

——— 1974. *Development in Infancy*. San Francisco: W. H. Freeman and Company.

——— 1977. *The Perceptual World of the Child*. Cambridge, Mass.: Harvard University Press.

Braine, M. D. S. 1959. "The Ontogeny of Certain Logical Operations: Piaget's Formulation Examined by Nonverbal Methods." *Psychological Monographs*, 73(5). Whole no. 475.

——— 1962. "Piaget on Reasoning: A Methodological Critique and Alternative Proposals." In W. Kessen and C. Kuhlman (Eds.), *Thought in the Young Child*. Monographs of the Society for Research in Child Development, 27 (2, Serial no. 83): 41–61.

——— 1964. "Development of a Grasp of Transitivity of Length: A Reply to Smedslund." *Child Development*, 35: 799–810.

Braine, M. D. S., and B. L. Shanks. 1965. "The Development of Conservation of Size." *Journal of Verbal Learning and Verbal Behavior*, 4: 227–242.

Brainerd, C. J., and S. H. Brainerd, 1972. "Order of Acquisition of Number and Quantity Conservation." *Child Development*, 43: 1901–1906.

Brison, D. W. 1966. "Acceleration of Conservation of Substance." *Journal of Genetic Psychology*, 109: 311–322.

Bruner, J. S. 1960. *The Process of Education*. New York: Vintage Books.

——— 1964. "The Course of Cognitive Development." *American Psychologist*, 19: 1–16.

——— 1965. "The Growth of Mind." *American Psychologist*, 20: 1007–1017.

——— 1966. *Toward a Theory of Instruction*. Cambridge, Mass.: Harvard University Press.

——— 1968. *Processes of Cognitive Growth in Infancy*. Heinz Werner Lectures, Clark University, Worcester. Vol. 3. Barre, Mass.: Barre.

——— 1972. "Nature and Uses of Immaturity." *American Psychologist*, 27: 1–22.

——— 1974. "The Organization of Early Skilled Action." In M. P. Richards (Ed.), *The Integration of the Child into a Social World*. New York: Cambridge University Press.

Bruner, J. S., R. R. Olver, and P. M. Greenfield. 1966. *Studies in Cognitive Growth.* New York: Wiley.

Bynum, T. W., J. A. Thomas, and L. J. Weitz. 1972. "Truthfunctional Logic in Formal Operational Thinking—Inhelder and Piaget's Evidence." *Developmental Psychology,* 7: 129–132.

Carey, S., and N. Block. 1973. "Should Philosophy and Psychology Remarry?" *Contemporary Psychology,* 18: 597–600. A review of T. Mischel (Ed.), *Cognitive Development and Epistemology.* New York: Academic Press.

Case, D., and J. M. Collinson. 1962. "The Development of Formal Thinking in Verbal Comprehension." *British Journal of Educational Psychology,* 57: 103–111.

Cole, M., J. Gay, J. A. Glick, and D. W. Sharp. 1971. *The Cultural Context of Learning and Thinking—An Exploration in Experimental Anthropology.* New York: Basic Books.

Cowan, P. A., J. Langer, J. Heavenrich, and M. Nathanson. 1969. "Social Learning and Piaget's Cognitive Theory of Moral Development." *Journal of Personality and Social Psychology,* 11: 261–274.

Dasen, P. R. "Cross-Cultural Piagetian Research—A Summary." *Journal of Cross-Cultural Psychology,* 3: 23–29.

Dodwell, P. C. 1960. "Children's Understanding of Number and Related Concepts." *Canadian Journal of Psychology,* 14: 191–205.

——— 1961. "Children's Understanding of Number Concepts: Characteristics of an Individual and of a Group Test." *Canadian Journal of Psychology,* 15: 29–36.

——— 1963. "Relations Between the Understanding of the Logic of Classes and of Cardinal Number in Children." *Canadian Journal of Psychology,* 16: 152–160.

Duckworth, E. 1972. "The Having of Wonderful Ideas." *Harvard Educational Review,* 42: 217–231.

——— 1973. "Language and Thought." In M. Schwebel and J. Raph (Eds.), *Piaget in the Classroom.* New York: Basic Books.

——— 1973. "Piaget Takes a Teacher's Look." *Learning,* 2: 22–27.

——— 1976. "And Some Comments on Learning to Spell." *Urban Review,* 9(2): 121–132.

Dudek, S. Z., E. P. Lester, J. S. Goldberg, and G. B. Dyer. 1969. "Relationship of Piaget Measures to Standard Intelligence and Motor Scales." *Perceptual and Motor Skills,* 28: 351–362.

Educational Testing Service. 1965. *Let's Look at First Graders—A Guide to Understanding and Fostering Intellectual Development in Young Children.* (Rev. ed.). New York: Board of Education of the City of New York.

———— 1965. *Written Exercises for First Graders—Manual of Directions.* New York: Board of Education of the City of New York.

Elkind, D. 1961. "The Development of Quantitative Thinking: A Systematic Replication of Piaget's Studies." *Journal of Genetic Psychology*, 98: 37–46.

———— 1961. "Children's Discovery of the Conservation of Mass, Weight, and Volume: Piaget Replication Study II." *Journal of Genetic Psychology*, 98: 219–227.

———— 1961. "The Development of the Additive Composition of Classes in the Child: Piaget Replication Study III." *Journal of Genetic Psychology*, 99: 51–57.

———— 1961. "Children's Conception of Right and Left: Piaget Replication Study IV." *Journal of Genetic Psychology*, 99: 269–276.

———— 1962. "Children's Conception of Brother and Sister: Piaget Replication Study V." *Journal of Genetic Psychology*, 100: 129–136.

———— 1964. "Discrimination, Seriation, and Numeration of Size and Dimensional Differences in Young Children: Piaget Replication Study VI." *Journal of Genetic Psychology*, 104: 275–296.

———— 1971. "Measuring Young Minds—Piaget." *Horizon*, 13(1): 33–37.

———— 1972. "What Does Piaget Say to the Teacher?" *Today's Education*, 61(8): 46–28.

———— 1974. *Children and Adolescence: Interpretive Essays on Jean Piaget.* (2nd ed.). New York: Oxford University Press.

———— 1976. "Elkind Updates Piaget." *Day Care and Early Education*, 4(1): 9–10.

———— 1978. "Understanding the Young Adolescent." *Adolescence*, 13(49): 127–134.

Elkind, D. and J. Flavell (Eds.). 1969. *Studies in Cognitive Development: Essays in Honor of Jean Piaget.* New York: Oxford University Press.

Fix, W. T., and J. W. Renner. 1979. "Chemistry and the Experiment in Secondary Schools." *Journal of Chemical Education*, 56(11): 737–740.

Flavell, J. H. 1963. *The Developmental Psychology of Jean Piaget.* Princeton, N.J.: D. Van Nostrand.

Furth, H. G. 1964. "Conservation of Weight in Deaf and Hearing Children." *Child Development,* 35: 143–150.

———— 1968. *Thinking Without Language—Psychological Implications of Deafness.* London: Collier-Macmillan.

———— 1968. "Piaget's Theory of Knowledge—The Nature of Representation and Interiorization." *Psychological Review,* 75: 143–154.

———— 1969. *Piaget and Knowledge—Theoretical Foundations.* Englewood Cliffs, N.J.: Prentice-Hall.

1970. *Piaget for Teachers.* Englewood Cliffs, N.J.: Prentice-Hall.

———— 1976. "Children's Conception of Social Institutions: A Piagetian Framework." *Human Development,* 19(6): 351–374.

Furth, H. G., and H. Wachs. 1974. *Thinking Goes to School—Piaget's Theory in Practice.* New York: Oxford University Press.

Furth, H. G., and J. Youniss. 1971. "Formal Operations and Language: A Comparison of Deaf and Hearing Adolescents." *International Journal of Psychology,* 6(1): 49–64.

Furth, H. G., J. Youniss, and B. M. Ross. 1970. "Children's Utilization of Logical Symbols—An Interpretation of Conceptual Behavior Based on Piagetian Theory." *Developmental Psychology,* 3: 36–57.

Gelman, R. 1969. "Conservation Acquisition—A Problem of Learning to Attend to Relevant Attributes." *Journal of Experimental Psychology,* 7: 167–187.

———— 1972. "The Nature and Development of Early Number Concepts." In H. W. Reese (Ed.), *Advances in Child Development and Behavior.* New York: Academic Press.

Ginsburg, H., and S. Opper (Eds.). 1979. *Piaget's Theory of Intellectual Development.* (2nd ed.). Englewood Cliffs, N.J.: Prentice-Hall.

Goldschmid, M. L., and P. M. Bentler. 1968. *Concept Assessment Kit—Conservation Manual.* San Diego, Calif.: Educational and Industrial Testing Service.

———— 1968. "The Dimensions and Measurement of Conservation." *Child Development,* 39: 787–802.

Goodnow, J. J. 1962. "A Test of Milieu Effects with Some of Piaget's Tasks." *Psychological Monographs,* 76(555): 1–22.

———— 1969. "Problems in Research on Culture and Thought." In D. Elkind and J. H. Flavell (Eds.), *Studies in Cognitive Development: Essays in Honor of Jean Piaget.* New York: Oxford University Press.

Goodnow, J. J., and G. Bethon. 1966. "Piaget's Tasks—The Effects of Schooling and Intelligence." *Child Development*, 37: 573–582.

Gratch, G. K. J. Appel, W. F. Evans, G. K. LeCompte, and N. A. Wright. 1974. "Piaget's Stage IV Object Concept Error—Evidence of Forgetting or Object Conception?" *Child Development*, 45: 71–77.

Green, D. R., M. P. Ford, and G. P. Flamer (Eds.). 1971. Measurement and Piaget. New York: McGraw-Hill.

Griffiths, J., C. Shantz, and I. E. Sigel. 1967. "A Methodological Problem in Conservation Studies: The Use of Relational Terms." *Child Development*, 38(3): 841–848.

Gruen, G. E. 1965. "Experiences Affecting the Development of Number Conservation in Children." *Child Development*, 36: 964–979.

Hall, E. "A Conversation with Jean Piaget." *Psychology Today*, 3: 25–32.

Harlow, H. F. 1949. "The Formation of Learning Sets." *Psychological Review*, 56: 51–65.

Hebb, D. O. 1949. *The Organization of Behavior*. New York: Wiley.

——— 1958 [1966]. *A Textbook of Psychology*. Philadelphia: Saunders.

High/Scope Educational Research Foundation. 1973. *The High/Scope Early Elementary Program—Cognitively Oriented Curriculum for Project Follow-Through, Grades K–3*. Ypsilanti, Mich.: High/Scope Educational Research Foundation.

——— 1974. *Early Childhood Education and Research—Report 1973*. Ypsilanti, Mich.: High/Scope Educational Research Foundation.

Hood, H. B. 1962. "An Experimental Study of Piaget's Theory of the Development of Number in Children." *British Journal of Psychology*, 53(3): 273–286.

Hunt, J. M. 1961. *Intelligence and Experience*. New York: Ronald Press.

——— 1963. "Piaget's Observations as a Source of Hypotheses Concerning Motivation." *Merrill-Palmer Quarterly*, 9: 263–275.

Inhelder, B. 1953. "Criteria of the Stages of Mental Development." In J. M. Tanner and B. Inhelder (Eds.), *Discussions on Child Development*. New York: International Universities Press.

——— 1965. "Operational Thought and Symbolic Imagery." In P. H. Mussen (Ed.), *European Research in Cognitive Development*. Monographs of the Society for Research in Child Development, 30(2): 4–18.

Inhelder, B., and J. Piaget. (1943) 1968. *Diagnosis of Reasoning in the Mentally Retarded.* Trans. W. B. Stephens. New York: Day.

———— 1959 [1964]. *The Early Growth of Logic in the Child: Classification and Seriation.* New York: Norton.

———— 1955 [1958]. *The Growth of Logical Thinking from Childhood to Adolescence: An Essay on the Construction of Formal Operational Structures.* Trans. A. Parsons and S. Milgram. New York: Basic Books.

Inhelder, B., and H. Sinclair. 1969. "Learning Cognitive Structures." In P. H. Mussen, J. Langer, and M. Covington (Eds.), *Trends and Issues in Developmental Psychology.* New York: Holt, Rinehart and Winston.

Inhelder, B., M. Bovet, H. Sinclair, and C. D. Smock. 1966. "On Cognitive Development." *American Psychologist,* 21: 160–165.

Irwin, M. D., and G. S. Moore. 1971. "The Young Child's Understanding of Social Justice." *Developmental Psychology,* 5: 406–410.

Jahoda, G. 1958. "Child Animism. I. A Critical Survey of Crosscultural Research. II. A Study in West Africa." *Journal of Social Psychology,* 47: 197–222.

Kamii, C. K. 1970. "Piaget's Theory and Specific Instruction—A Response to Bereiter and Kohlberg." *Interchange,* 1: 33–39.

———— 1971. "Evaluation of Learning in Preschool Education—Sociocmotional, Perceptual-Motor, and Cognitive Development." In B. S. Bloom, J. T. Hastings, and G. F. Madaus (Eds.), *Handbook of Formative and Summative Evaluation of Student Learning.* New York: McGraw-Hill.

———— 1972. "An Application of Piaget's Theory to the Conceptualization of a Preschool Curriculum." In R. K. Parker (Ed.), *The Preschool in Action.* Boston: Allyn & Bacon.

———— 1972. "A Sketch of the Piaget-Derived Preschool Curriculum Developed by the Ypsilanti Early Education Program." In S. Braun and E. Edwards (Eds.), *History and Theory of Early Childhood Education.* Worthington, Ohio: Jones. [Also available in J. Frost (Ed.), 1973, *Revisiting Early Childhood Education* (New York: Holt, Rinehart and Winston); and in B. Spodek (Ed.), 1973, *Early Childhood Education* (Englewood Cliffs, N.J.: Prentice-Hall).]

———— 1979. "Piaget's Theory, Behaviorism, and Other Theories in Education." *Journal of Education,* 161: 13–33.

Kamii, C. K., and L. Derman. 1971. "The Englemann Approach to Teaching Logical Thinking: Findings from the Administration of Some Piagetian Tasks." In D. R. Green, M. P. Ford, and G. B. Flamer (Eds.), *Measurement and Piaget.* New York: McGraw-Hill.

Kamii, C. K., and R. DeVries. 1976. *Piaget, Children, and Number.* Washington, D.C.: National Association for the Education of Young Children.

——— 1977. "Piaget for Early Education." In M. C. Day and R. K. Parker (Eds.), *The Preschool in Action.* (2nd ed.). Boston: Allyn & Bacon.

——— 1978. *Physical Knowledge in Preschool Education: Implications of Piaget's Theory.* Englewood Cliffs, N.J.: Prentice-Hall, 1978.

——— 1980. *Group Games in Early Education: Implications of Piaget's Theory.* Washington, D.C.: National Association for the Education of Young Children.

Kamii, C. K., and L. Lee-Katz. 1979. "Physics in Preschool Education: A Piagetian Approach." *Young Children,* 34: 4–9.

Kamii, C. K., and N. L. Radin. 1967. "A Framework for a Preschool Curriculum Based on Some Piagetian Concepts." *Journal of Creative Behavior,* 1: 314–324.

——— 1970. "A Framework for a Preschool Curriculum Based on Piaget's Theory." In I. J. Athey and D. O. Rubadeau (Eds.), *Educational Implications of Piaget's Theory.* Waltham, Mass.: Ginn-Blaisdell.

Karplus, E. F., and R. Karplus. 1970. "Intellectual Development Beyond Elementary School. I. Deductive Logic." *School Science and Mathematics,* 70: 398–406.

Karplus, R., and E. F. Karplus. 1972. "Intellectual Development Beyond Elementary School. III. Ratio—A Longitudinal Study." *School Science and Mathematics,* 72: 735–742.

Karplus, R., and R. W. Peterson. 1970. "Intellectual Development Beyond Elementary School. II. Ratio—A Survey." *School Science and Mathematics,* 70: 813–820.

Kaufman, A. S. 1971. "Piaget and Gesell—A Psychometric Analysis of Tests Built from Their Tasks." *Child Development,* 42: 1341–1360.

Kaufman, A. S., and N. L. Kaufman. 1972. "Tests Built from Piaget's and Gesell's Tasks as Predictors of First-Grade Achievement." *Child Development,* 43: 521–535.

Kendler, T. S. 1963. "Development of Mediating Responses in Children." *Monographs of the Society for Research in Child Development,* 28: 33–48.

Kephart, N. C. 1960. *The Slow Learner in the Classroom.* Columbus, Ohio: Merrill.

———— 1968. *Learning Disability.* West Lafayette, Ind.: Kappa Delta Pi Press.

Kofsky, E. 1966. "A Scalogram Study of Classificatory Development." *Child Development,* 37: 191–204.

Kohlberg, L. 1968. "The Child as Moral Philosopher." *Psychology Today,* 2: 24–30.

———— 1968. "Early Education—A Cognitive-Developmental View." *Child Development,* 39: 1013–1062.

———— 1973. "Moral Development and the New Social Studies." *Social Education,* 37(5): 369–375.

Kohlberg, L., and C. Gilligan. 1971. "The Adolescent as a Philosopher—The Discovery of the Self in a Postconventional World." *Daedalus,* 100: 1051–1084.

Kohlberg, L., and P. Whitten. 1972. "Understanding the Hidden Curriculum." *Learning,* 1(2): 10–19.

Kohler, W. 1924 [1959]. *The Mentality of Apes.* Trans. (from 2nd rev. ed.) E. Winter. New York: Vintage Books.

Kohnstamm, G. A. 1963. "An Evaluation of Part of Piaget's Theory." *Acta Psychologica,* 1: 313–356.

Lambie, D. Z., J. T. Bond, and D. P. Weikart. 1974. *Infants, Mothers and Teachering—A Study of Infant Education and Home Visits.* Summary of Final Report, Ypsilanti Carnegie Infant Education Project. Ypsilanti, Mich.: High/Scope Educational Research Foundation.

Langer, J. 1969. "Disequilibrium as a Source of Development." In P. H. Mussen, J. Langer, and M. Covington (Eds.), *Trends and Issues in Developmental Psychololgy.* New York: Holt, Rinehart and Winston.

———— 1974/1975. "Interactional Aspects of Cognitive Organization." *Cognition,* 3(1): 9–28.

Langer, J., and S. Strauss. 1972. "Appearance, Reality, and Identity." *Cognition,* 1: 105–128.

Lavatelli, C. 1970. *Early Childhood Curriculum—A Piaget Program.* Boston: American Science and Engineering.

———— 1970. *Teacher's Guide to Accompany* "Early Childhood Curriculum—A Piaget Program." Boston: American Science and Engineering.

———— 1971. *A Piaget Preschool Program in Action, I and II. Number, Measurement, and Space.* Little Neck, N.Y.: Knowledge Tree Films.

Lawson, A. E., and J. W. Renner. 1974. "A Quantitative Analysis of Responses to Piagetian Tasks and Its Implications for Curriculum." *Science Education,* 58(4), 454–559.

———— 1975. "Piagetian Theory and Biology Teaching." *American Biology Teacher,* 37(6), 336–343.

———— 1975. "Relationships of Science Subject Matter and Developmental Levels of Learners." *Journal of Research in Science Teaching,* 12(4), 347–358.

Lovell, K. 1959. "A Follow-Up Study of Some Aspects of the Work of Piaget and Inhelder on the Child's Conception of Space." *British Journal of Educational Psychology,* 29: 104–117.

———— 1961. "A Follow-Up Study of Inhelder and Piaget's 'The Growth of Logical Thinking,' " *British Journal of Educational Psychology,* 52: 143–153.

———— 1961. *The Growth of Basic Mathematical and Scientific Concepts in Children.* London: University of London Press.

Lovell, K., and A. Slater. 1960. "The Growth of the Concept of Time: A Comparative Study." *Journal of Child Psychology and Psychiatry,* 1: 179–190.

Lovell, K., B. Mitchell, and I. R. Everett. 1962. "An Experimental Study of the Growth of Some Logical Structures." *British Journal of Educational Psychology,* 53(2): 175–188.

Lunzer, E. A. 1960. "Some Points of Piagetian Theory in Light of Experimental Criticism." *Journal of Child Psychology and Psychiatry,* 1: 191–200.

———— 1960. *Recent Studies in Britain Based on the Work of Jean Piaget.* London: National Foundation of Educational Research in England and Wales.

———— 1970. "Construction of a Standardized Battery of Piagetian Tests to Assess the Development of Effective Intelligence." *Research in Education,* 3: 53–72.

Lunzer, E. A., and others. 1976. "The Distinctiveness of Operativity as a Measure of Cognitive Functioning in Five-Year-Old Children." *British Journal of Educational Psychology,* 46(3): 280–295.

McKinnon, J. W., and J. W. Renner. 1971. "Are Colleges Concerned with Intellectual Development?" *American Journal of Physics*, 39: 1047–1052.

Morgan, J. J. B., and J. T. Morton. 1944. "The Distortion of Syllogistic Reasoning Produced by Personal Convictions." *Journal of Social Psychology*, 20: 39–59.

Nucci, L., and E. Turiel. 1976. "Social Interactions and the Development of Social Concepts in Pre-School Children." Paper presented at the Western Psychological Association Convention, Los Angeles, California, April 8–11.

O'Bryan, K. G., and R. S. MacArthur. 1967. "A Factor-Analytic Study of Piagetian Reversibility." *Alberta Journal of Educational Research*, 13: 211–220.

Piaget, J. 1923 [1926]. *The Language and Thought of the Child*. Trans. M. Worden. New York: Harcourt, Brace & World.

―――― 1924 [1928]. *Judgment and Reasoning in the Child*. Trans. M. Worden. New York: Harcourt, Brace & World.

―――― 1926 [1929]. *The Child's Conception of the World*. Trans. J. Tomlinson and A. Tomlinson. New York: Routledge & Kegan Paul.

―――― 1927 [1930]. *The Child's Conception of Physical Causality*. Trans. M. Worden. New York: Harcourt, Brace & World.

―――― 1932. *The Moral Judgment of the Child*. Trans. M. Worden. New York: Harcourt, Brace & World.

―――― 1936 [1952]. *The Origins of Intelligence in Children*. Trans. M. Cook. New York: International Universities Press.

―――― 1937 [1954]. *The Construction of Reality in the Child*. Trans. M. Cook. New York: Basic Books.

―――― 1941 [1952]. *The Child's Conception of Number*. Trans. C. Gattegno and F. M. Hodgson. New York: Norton.

―――― 1945 [1951]. *Play, Dreams, and Imitation in Childhood*. Trans. C. Gattegno and F. M. Hodgson. New York: Norton.

―――― 1946 [1970]. *The Child's Conception of Movement and Speed*. Trans. G. E. T. Holloway and M. J. Mackenzie. London: Routledge & Kegan Paul.

―――― 1946 [1969]. *The Child's Conception of Time*. Trans. A. J. Pomerans. London: Routledge & Kegan Paul.

―――― 1947 [1950]. *The Psychology of Intelligence*. Trans. M. Piercy and D. E. Berlyne. London: Routledge & Kegan Paul.

———— 1952. "Jean Piaget." In E. G. Boring, H. S. Langfeld, H. Werner, and R. M. Yerkes (Eds.), *A History of Psychology in Autobiography*. Worcester, Mass.: Clark University Press.

———— 1953. "How Children Form Mathematical Concepts." *Scientific American*, 189(5), 74–79. (Offprint 420.)

———— 1955. "The Development of Time Concepts in the Child." In R. H. Hoch and J. Zubin (Eds.), *Psychopathology of Childhood*. New York: Grune & Stratton.

———— 1952 [1957]. *Logic and Psychology*. New York: Basic Books.

———— 1957. "The Child and Modern Physics." *Scientific American*, 196(3): 46–51.

———— 1959. *Bulletin Psychologique*, Paris, 12, 538–540, 574–576, 724–727, 806–807, 857–860.

———— 1964. "Development and Learning." In R. E. Ripple and V. N. Rockcastle (Eds.), *Piaget Rediscovered*. Ithaca, N.Y.: Cornell University Press.

———— 1964. "Cognitive Development in Children: Piaget Development and Learning." *Journal of Research in Science Teaching*, 2: 176–186.

———— 1964 [1967]. *Six Psychological Studies*. Trans. A. Tenzer. Ed. D. Elkind. New York: Random House.

———— 1967 [1971]. *Biology and Knowledge*. Chicago: University of Chicago Press.

———— 1967. *On the Development of Memory and Identity*. Heinz Werner Lectures, Clark University, Worcester. Vol. 2. Barre, Mass.: Barre.

———— 1968 [1970]. *Structuralism*. Trans. C. Maschler. New York: Basic Books.

———— 1935/1969 [1970]. *Science of Education and the Psychology of the Child*. Trans. D. Coltman. New York: Orion Press.

———— 1970. *Genetic Epistemology*. Trans. E. Duckworth. New York: Columbia University Press.

———— 1972. "Problems of Equilibration." In C. F. Nadine, J. M. Gallagher, and R. D. Humphries (Eds.), *Piaget and Inhelder: On Equilibration*. Philadelphia: Jean Piaget Society.

———— 1970 [1972]. *The Principles of Genetic Epistemology*. Trans. W. Mays. London: Routledge & Kegan Paul.

———— 1970 [1971]. *Psychology and Epistemology*. Trans. A. Rosin. New York: Grossman.

—— 1966 (1971). *Mental Imagery in the Child—A Study of the Development of Imaginal Representation.* Trans. P. A. Chilton. New York: Basic Books.

—— 1971. "The Theory of Stages in Cognitive Development." In D. R. Green, M. P. Ford, and G. B. Flamer (Eds.), *Measurement and Piaget.* New York: McGraw-Hill.

—— 1948/1971 [1973]. *To Understand Is to Invent—The Future of Education.* New York: Grossman.

—— 1972 [1973]. *The Child and Reality—Problems of Genetic Psychololgy.* Trans. A. Rosin. New York: Grossman.

—— 1972. "Intellectual Evolution from Adolescence to Adulthood." *Human Development,* 15(1): 1–12.

—— 1972. "Physical World of the Child." *Physics Today,* 25(6): 23–27.

—— 1972. "A Structural Foundation for Tomorrow's Education." *Prospects,* 2(1): 12–27.

—— 1974. "The Future of Developmental Child Psychology." *Journal of Youth and Adolescence,* 3(2): 87–94.

—— 1975. "Comments on Mathematical Education." *Contemporary Education,* 47(1): 5–10.

—— 1975. "From Noise to Order: The Psychological Development of Knowledge and Phenocopy in Biology." *Urban Review,* 8(3): 209–218.

—— 1975 [1977]. *The Development of Thought: Equilibration of Cognitive Structures.* New York: Viking Press.

—— 1976. "Coordination-Integration, Equilibration and Intervention for Cognitive Change." *Contemporary Psychology,* 21(3): 226–227.

Piaget, J., and B. Inhelder. 1947. "Diagnosis of Mental Operations and Theory of Intelligence." *American Journal of Mental Deficiency,* 51(3): 401–406.

—— 1948 [1956]. *The Child's Conception of Space.* Trans. F. J. Langdon and J. L. Lunzer. New York: Norton.

—— 1959. *La Genese des Structures Logiques Elementaire: Classifications et Seriations.* Neuchâtel: Delachaux et Niestlé.

—— 1966 [1969]. *The Psychology of the Child.* Trans. H. Weaver. New York: Basic Books.

—— 1969. "The Gaps in Empiricism." In A. Koestler (Ed.), *Beyond Reductionism.* New York: Hutchinson.

—— 1968 [1972]. *Memory and Intelligence*. Trans. A. J. Pomerans. New York: Basic Books.

Piaget, J., B. Inhelder, and A. Szeminska. 1948 [1960]. *The Child's Conception of Geometry*. Trans. E. A. Lunzer. New York: Basic Books.

Pinard, A., and G. Chasse. 1977. "Pseudoconservation of the Volume and Surface Area of a Solid Object." *Child Development*, 48(4): 1559–1566.

Pinard, A., and M. Laurendeau. 1964. "A Scale of Mental Development Based on Piaget's Theory." *Journal of Research in Science Teaching*, 2: 253–260.

—— 1969. " 'Stage' in Piaget's Cognitive-Developmental Theory— Exegesis of a Concept." In D. Elkind and J. H. Flavell (Eds.), *Studies in Cognitive Development: Essays in Honor of Jean Piaget*. New York: Oxford University Press.

Renner, J. W. 1976. "Significant Physics Content and Intellectual Development." *Physics Education*, 11: 458–462.

—— 1979. "The Relationships Between Intellectual Development and Written Responses to Science Questions." *Journal of Research in Science Teaching*, 16(4): 279–299.

Renner, J. W., and R. M. Grant. 1978. "Can Students Grasp Physics Concepts?" *Science Teacher*, 45(7): 30–33.

Renner, J. W., and A. E. Lawson. 1973. "Piagetian Theory and Instruction in Physics." *Physics Teacher*, 11: 273–276.

—— 1973. "Promoting Intellectual Development Through Science Teaching." *Physics Teacher*, 37: 55–57.

Renner, J. W., and J. A. Nickel. 1979. "Physics and the Experiment in the Secondary Schools." *Physics Teacher*, 17(2): 115–116.

Renner, J. W., and W. C. Paske. 1977. "Quantitative Competencies of College Students." *Journal of College Science Teaching*, 6(5): 283–292.

—— 1977. "Comparing Two Forms of Instruction in College Physics." *American Journal of Physics*, 45(9): 851–859.

Renner, J. W., and D. G. Phillips. 1980. "Piaget's Developmental Model: A Basis for Research in Science Education." *School Science and Mathematics*, 80(2): 193–198.

Renner, J. W., and D. G. Stafford, 1970. "Inquiry, Children and Teachers." *Science Teacher*, 37: 55–57.

—— 1972. *Teaching Science in the Secondary School*. New York: Harper & Row.

Renner, J. W., R. M. Grant, and J. Sutherland. 1978. "Content and Concrete Thought." *Science Education*, 62(2): 215–221.

Renner, J. W., J. Brock, S. Heath, M. Laughlin, and J. Stevens. 1971. "Piaget IS Practical." *Science and Children*, 9: 23–26.

Renner, J. W., D. G. Stafford, W. J. Coffia, D. H. Kellogg, and M. C. Weber. 1973. "An Evaluation of the Science Curriculum Improvement Study." *School Science and Mathematics*, 73: 291–318.

Ripple, R. E., and V. N. Rockcastle (Eds.). 1964. "Piaget Rediscovered: Selected Papers from a Conference on Cognitive Studies and Curriculum Development." *Journal of Research in Science Teaching*, 2(3): 187–195.

Rosenthal, R., and K. L. Fade. 1963. "The Effect of Experimenter Bias on the Performance of the Albino Rat." *Behavioral Science*, 8: 183–189.

Rosenthal, R., and L. Jacobson. 1968. *Pygmalion in the Classroom*. New York: Holt, Rinehart and Winston.

Rosenthal, R., and R. Lawson. 1964. "A Longitudinal Study of Experimenter Bias on the Operant Learning of Laboratory Rats." *Journal of Psychiatric Research*, 2: 61–72.

Ross, R. J. 1973. "Some Empirical Parameters of Formal Thinking." *Journal of Youth and Adolescence*, 2: 167–177.

———— 1974. "The Empirical Status of the Formal Operations." *Adolescence*, 9: 413–420.

Schwebel, M., and J. Raph. *Piaget in the Classroom*. New York: Basic Books.

Sigel, I. E. 1953. "Developmental Trends in the Abstraction Ability of Children." *Child Development*, 24: 131–144.

———— 1964. "The Attainment of Concepts." In M. L. Hoffman and L. V. Hoffman (Eds.), *Review of Child Development Research*. Vol. 1. New York: Russell Sage Foundation.

Sigel, I. E., and F. H. Hooper (Eds.). 1968. *Logical Thinking in Children: Research Based on Piaget's Theory*. New York: Holt, Rinehart and Winston.

Sigel, I. E., A. Roeper, and F. H. Hooper. 1966. "A Training Procedure for Acquisition of Piaget's Conservation of Quantity: A Pilot Study and Its Replication." *British Journal of Educational Psychology*, 36: 301–311. [Reprinted in I. E. Sigel and F. H. Hooper (Eds.), 1968. *Logical Thinking in Children: Research* Based on Piaget's Theory (New York: Holt, Rinehart and Winston).]

Sigel, I. E., E. Saltz, and W. Roskind. 1967. "Variables Determining Concept Conservation." *Journal of Experimental Psychology*, 7: 471–475.

Slobin, D. I. 1973. "Cognitive Prerequisite for the Development of Grammar." In C. A. Ferguson and D. I. Slobin (Eds.), *Studies of Child Language Development*. New York: Holt, Rinehart and Winston.

Smedslund, J. 1961. "The Acquisition of Conservation of Substance and Weight in Children. I. Introduction." *Scandinavian Journal of Psychology*, 2: 11–20.

———— 1961. "The Acquisition of Conservation of Substance and Weight in Children. II. External Reinforcement of Conservation of Weight and the Operations of Additions and Subtractions." *Scandinavian Journal of Psychology*, 2: 71–84.

———— 1961. "The Acquisition of Conservation of Substance and Weight in Children. III. Extinction of Conservation of Weight Acquired 'Normally' and by Means of Empirical Controls on a Balance." *Scandinavian Journal of Psychology*, 2: 85–87.

———— 1961. "The Acquisition of Conservation of Substance and Weight in Children. IV. Attempt at Extinction of the Visual Components of the Weight Concept." *Scandinavian Journal of Psychology*, 2: 153–155.

———— 1961. "The Acquisition of Conservation of Substance and Weight in Children. V. Practice in Conflict Situations Without External Reinforcement." *Scandinavian Journal of Psychology*, 2: 156–160.

———— 1961. "The Acquisition of Conservation of Substance and Weight in Children. VI. Practice on Continuous vs. Discontinuous Material in Problem Situations Without External Reinforcement." *Scandinavian Journal of Psychology*, 2: 203–210.

———— 1962. "The Acquisition of Conservation of Substance and Weight in Children. VII. Conservation of Discontinuous Quantity and the Operations of Adding and Taking Away." *Scandinavian Journal of Psychology*, 3: 69–77.

———— 1963. "The Effect of Observation on Children's Representation of the Spatial Orientation of a Water Surface." *Journal of Genetic Psychology*, 102: 195–201.

———— 1963. "Development of Concrete Transitivity of Length in Children." *Child Development*, 34: 389–405.

—— 1964. "Concrete Reasoning—A Study of Intellectual Development." *Monographs of the Society for Research in Child Development*, 29(2), Series 93: 1–39.

—— 1965. "The Development of Transitivity of Length—A Comment on Braine's Reply." *Child Development*, 36: 577–580.

Sonquist, H., and C. K. Kamii. 1967. "Applying Some Piagetian Concepts in the Classroom for the Disadvantaged." *Young Children*, 22: 231–246.

Sonquist, H., C. K. Kamii, and L. Derman. 1970. "A Piaget-Derived Preschool Curriculum." In I. J. Athey and D. O. Rubadeau (Eds.), *Educational Implications of Piaget's Theory*. Waltham, Mass.: Ginn-Blaisdell.

Stephens, W. B., C. K. Miller, and J. A. McLaughlin. 1969. *The Development of Reasoning, Moral Judgment, and Moral Conduct in Retardates and Normals*. Report on Project No. RD-2382-P. Philadelphia: Temple University Press.

Stephens, W. B., J. A. McLaughlin, C. K. Miller, and G. V. Glass. 1962. "The Factorial Structure of Reasoning, Moral Judgment, and Moral Conduct." *Developmental Psychology*, 6: 343–348.

Strauss, S., and J. Langer. 1970. "Operational Thought Inducement." *Child Development*, 41: 163–175.

Suchman, J. R. 1964. "The Illinois Studies in Inquiry Training." *Journal of Research in Science Teaching*, 2: 231–232.

Szeminska, A. 1965. "The Evolution of Thought: Some Applications of Research Findings to Educational Practice." In P. H. Mussen (Ed.), *European Research in Cognitive Development*. Monographs of the Society for Research in Child Development, 30(2): 47–57.

Tanner, J. M., and B. Inhelder (Eds.). 1960. *The Proceedings of the World Health Organization Study Group on the Psychological Development of the Child. Geneva, 1956. Vol. 4: Discussions on Child Development: A Consideration of the Biological, Psychological, and Cultural Approaches to the Understanding of Human Development and Behavior*. New York: International Universities Press.

Tuddenham, R. D. 1966. "Jean Piaget and the World of the Child." *American Psychologist*, 21: 207–217.

Turiel, E., and G. Rothman. 1972. "The Influence of Reasoning on Behavioral Choices at Different Stages of Moral Development." *Child Development*, 43: 741–756.

Vernon, P. E. 1965. "Environmental Handicaps and Intellectual Development." *British Journal of Educational Psychology*, 35: 9–20, 117–126.

——— "Educational and Intellectual Development Among Canadian Indians and Eskimos." *Educational Review*, 18: 79–91, 186–195.

Warburton, F. W. 1969. "The British Intelligence Scale." In W. B. Dockrell (Ed.), *On Intelligence*. The Toronto Symposium on Intelligence. London: Methuen.

Weikart, D., L. Rogers, C. Adcock, and D. McClelland. 1971. *The Cognitively Oriented Curriculum—A Framework for Preschool Teachers*. Urbana: University of Illinois Press.

White, B. L. 1967. "An Experimental Approach to the Effects of Experience on Early Human Behavior." In J. P. Hill (Ed.), *Minnesota Symposium on Child Psychology*. Vol. 1. Minneapolis: University of Minnesota Press.

White, B. L., and R. Held. 1966. "Plasticity of Sensorimotor Development in the Human Infant." In J. F. Rosenblith and W. Alinsmith (Eds.), *The Causes of Behavior: Readings in Child Development and Educational Psychology*. (2nd ed.). Boston: Allyn & Bacon.

Wohlwill, J. F. 1960. "Developmental Studies of Perception." *Psychological Bulletin*, 57: 249–288.

——— 1960. "A Study of the Development of the Number Concept by Scalogram Analysis." *Journal of Genetic Psychology*, 97: 345–377.

——— 1963. "Piaget's System as a Source of Empirical Research." *Merrill-Palmer Quarterly*, 9: 253–262.

——— 1964. "Cognitive Development and the Learning of Elementary Concepts." *Journal of Research in Science Teaching*, 2: 222, 226.

——— 1966. "Comments in Discussion on the Developmental Approach of Jean Piaget." *American Journal of Mental Deficiency*, (Monograph Supplement), 70: 84–105.

——— 1966. "Piaget's Theory of the Development of Intelligence in the Concrete Operations Period." *American Journal of Mental Deficiency* (Monograph Supplement), 70: 57–83.

——— 1967. "The Mystery of the Prelogical Child." *Psychology Today*, 1: 25–34.

——— 1975. "Children's Responses to Meaningful Pictures Varying in Diversity: Exploration Time vs. Preference." *Journal of Experimental Child Psychology*, 20(2): 341–351.

Wohlwill, J. F., and R. C. Lowe. 1962. "Experimental Analysis of the Development of the Conservation of Number." *Child Development*, 33: 153–168.

Woodward, M. "The Behavior of Idiots Interpreted by Piaget's Theory of Sensori-Motor Development." *British Journal of Educational Psychology*, 29: 60–71.

——— "Concepts of Number of the Mentally Subnormal Studied by Piaget's Method." *Journal of Child Psychology and Psychiatry*, 2: 249–259.

——— 1962. "Concepts of Space in the Mentally Subnormal Studied by Piaget's Method." *British Journal of Social and Clinical Psychology*, 1: 25–37.

Youniss, J., H. G. Furth, and B. M. Ross. 1971. "Logical Symbol Use in Deaf and Hearing Children and Adolescents." *Developmental Psychology*, 5: 511–517.

Index

187